Shop windows

SHOP WINDOWS

RotoVision SA

AUTHOR
Francisco Asensio Cerver

EDITOR IN CHIEF
Paco Asensio

PROJECT COORDINATOR
Rosa Maria Prats

PROOFREADING
Tobias Willett

TRANSLATION
A.B.C. Traduccions

© Copyright for International Edition
AXIS BOOKS, S.A.

© Copyright for English Edition
ROTOVISION

ISBN: 0-8230-6472-7

All rights reserved. The total or partial reproduction of this publication in any form or by any electrical or mechanical means; including photocopying, recording or by any information storage and retrieval system, or other wise: and the distribution of copies of the same through public rental or loan, are stricly prohibeted under the copyright law without the prior permission in writing of the holder of the copyright.

Shop Windows

8   Introduction

48   Byblos *Giorgio Longoni*

52   Jigsaw *Nigel Coates (Branson Coates Architecture)*

56   Adriana Mode *Gigi Bolzoni & Vanna Brega*

60   Loewe *Itziar Esteban-Infantes & Gustavo Torner*

64   Loja das Meias *Carlos Tojal (T&T Arquitectos)*

68   Trau *Estudio de Diseño y Decoración G.C.A.*

72   Ana Salazar *Ana Salazar*

76   Esprit *Treitl & Steffel (Sottsass Associati)*

80   L'Observatoire *Zébu*

84   Margarita Nuez *Oriol Armengou*

88   Tehen *Denis Colomb*

94   Alexander *Wolfgang Graswander*

100	JEAN-CHARLES DE CASTELBAJAC	*Patrick de Maupeou*
104	GIANFRANCO FERRÉ	*Letizia Caruzzo, Paolo C. Rancati & Ezio Riva, Architetti Associati*
110	LONDON HOUSE	*Federico Correa*
116	FUJIWARA	*Shimizu, Hisada & Sato*
120	HENRY COTTON'S	*Olivier Billiotte*
124	GIAN MARCO VENTURI	*Anna Clerici & Maddalena de Molinari*
128	LOFT	*Patrick Frêche*
132	GALTRUCCO	*Piero Pinto*
136	ARAMIS	*Mario Framis & Juan Flores*
140	CENTIMETRE	*Cezar Rinalducci*
144	REPLAY	*Stefania Leonardi & Rodolfo Dacomo*
148	OLIVIER STRELLI	*Michèle Kuborn*
152	EMPORIO ARMANI	*Giancarlo Ortelli*
156	AZUL	*Isabel García Tapia*

Introduction

The shop window of the Chipie youth fashion shop, in Paris, with one model of footwear displayed in all its different colours.

A view of the shop window of a boutique in which complementary accessories are on display, featuring an ethnic inspiration both in terms of the articles themselves and the decor.

INTRODUCTION TO THE CONCEPT OF THE SHOP WINDOW DISPLAY. DEFINITION, NECESSARY REQUIREMENTS AND QUALITIES

To attract, display, exhibit, promote, seduce and, finally, to sell; to sell a product or to sell an image. All of this is what is usually expected of this space located at the entrances to shops and commercial centres and bearing the generic name of shop window. The Oxford Dictionary definition is: "A window of a shop in which goods are displayed for sale." And figuratively as "A display of anything, resembling the display of goods by a tradesman, intended to catch the attention." The shop window is an enclosed space visible through the glass window, with a means of access, which may be either through a sliding front window or some kind of door communicating with the interior of the shop. It has between one and four glass walls enclosing the space which constitute the distinct view points which are available to the observer.

The shop window conceived merely as a space piled up with a few of the goods which are for sale does not exactly satisfy the objectives which it is expected to meet. A good shop window must be aimed at instilling the desire to buy in the person who contemplates it, and this can be achieved by means of a psychologically calculated display in which aesthetics, originality, dynamics and intention play an important role. It is not just a matter of displaying products, but

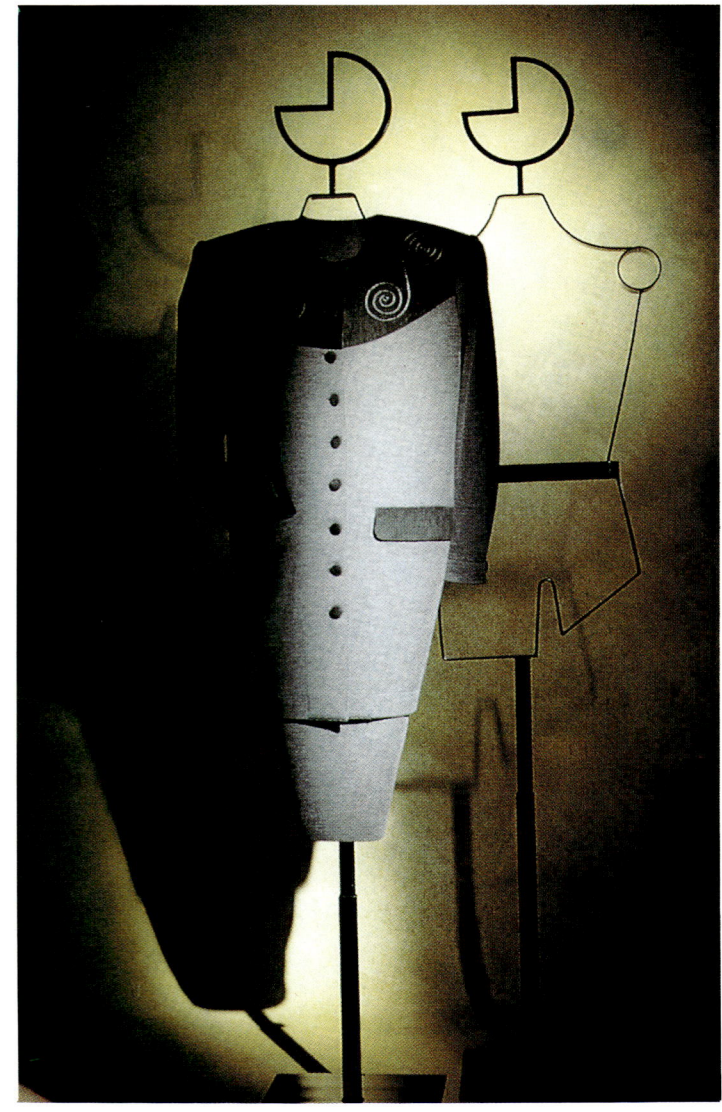

Mannequins are of great importance in all fashion centre shop window displays; a great diversity of effects can be achieved by the use of mannequins: stiffness, coolness and immobility, or conversely, the suggestion of dynamic movement.

On the following page, below, a shop window of a classical furniture shop, decorated according to criteria of harmony and balance.

Exterior view of a boutique with a shop window which is of the type "Shop as window display", that is where the whole of the premises, including the interior, can be seen by the public from the street, thus becoming its own advertisement.

The Thierry Mugler Shop in Paris, with its shop window dominated by the dynamic sense inspired by the four mannequins at the entrance.

Ladies' fashion boutique, lit at night (on the left) and during the day; it is important to take care of the look of the window when there is no natural light through the use of lighting which highlights both the interior and the façade.

The window display is also a fundamental part of any furniture shop.

11

On this page and the next, three proposals for a footwear shop window display: order, aesthetics, style, lighting and image can be conjugated in a variety of different ways to achieve effects as diverse as those in the photographs.

of attracting potential buyers to look at the window, which becomes the reflection of the personality of the shop and a kind of silent salesman.

The arrangement of the goods in a shop window in this special way is for some a technique and for others an art form, which goes by the name of window dressing. Whichever is the case it must respond to the demands of advanced sales techniques, be in tune with the socio-cultural environment of the country concerned and with both its traditional and avant-garde artistic tendencies.

Shop window dressing has its place within the reference framework of visual promotion, this being understood as a system of image projection based on visual means and aimed at the promotion of the attractive and desirable image of a product so as to awaken a sense of satisfaction and identification in the consumer. Shop window dressing and visual promotion are part and parcel of another discipline, that of advertising technique, given that the end is essentially a commercial one.

QUALITIES OF A SHOP WINDOW

The shop window may adopt highly diverse forms, in terms of design or as a result of structural and positional conditions, but whatever that form might be there are a series of qualities which must be satisfied in order that the ends can be achieved with any guarantee of success.

The whole must reflect the philosophy of the product in such a way that it exercises a powerful seductive influence, through a style that is identified with the idea of the brand name. Seen from this perspective the shop window is a component of manipulation through which an ideology and the aesthetics inherent in that ideology can also be reflected.

Its function, however, is not limited to displaying, seducing and attracting. It also implicitly bears the social responsibility of contributing to the embellishment of the city, although this must be subject to the commercial ends, which has its own importance in that it conditions aspects of quality such as the sense of modernity and a cultural and aesthetic suitability. These, then, are aspects which are independent of the priorities imposed by commercial ends, and which convert the act of going shopping into pleasure and entertainment which go much further than the simple search for the required goods.

In this context the product becomes a secondary element, the acquisition of which has more to do with the attractiveness and subtlety of the presentation than with the product

On the previous page, design and simplicity are the predominant notes in the shop window of Jacqueline Peres in Paris.
Classical art and the avant-garde are combined in this shoe shop window. In the lower photo the trademark of a fashion shop on the access door to the premises.

itself. Many years have passed since the basis of Western commerce lay in the satisfaction of man's essential needs, and the satisfaction of his secondary needs became the principal market mover. It is in this sphere that shop window dressing has adopted its role as the protagonist, an unquestionably effective weapon of seduction, which unleashes the primary impulses of consumerism, both in terms of the goods and of the image.

BASIC REQUIREMENTS

There are a series of technical and aesthetic conditions which every shop window must meet in order to fulfil its function effectively:

Visibility: of the different elements which make up the shop window; whether they be products, displays, price tags, photographs, etc.; in general the greater the perspective and the wider the visual angle, the better the visibility will be. The arrangement of the objects and the lighting also have an influence, which is vital for the creation of atmosphere and for the highlighting of colours and textures, or simply of specific articles.

On this and the previous page, two examples of shop windows in which the criteria of simplicity and harmony are the predominant note.

Two examples of perfumer's shop window displays in which the arrangement of the products evoke single geometric figures, a triangle (left) and a semicircle (right).

On this page, examples of compositional harmony in the shop windows of two jeweller's shops, in which simplicity is combined with a sense of classical elegance.

Conversely, on the following page, a degree of chaos reigns in the distribution of the books, the result being, at first sight at least, a certain difficulty in differentiating the products.

Coherence and unity: of the shop window and the façade, and of the different elements which make up the image of the shop, such as: the doorway, the trademark, decorative posters and exterior lighting. It is a matter of achieving a general balance based on an overall harmony.

Organisation: of the different elements which make up the shop window display, based on an order which encourages the act of observation on the part of the passers by, motivating them and, at the same time, reflecting the image of the particular style of the shop.

Plastic composition: guided by a creativity inspired in balance or tension, in static or dynamic expression, in the classical or the avant-garde; in short, giving shape to the style which the shop wishes to get across.

Opportuneness: consists in achieving the right coincidence between the shop window and the time of year, the fashion season, or even a specific day (such as St. Valentine's Day), in such a way that the shop window responds to the expectations of the public.

Attractiveness: the instilling of desire in the potential purchaser through the use of aesthetic and motivational means.

Originality and surprise: aimed at attracting the attention of the passers by.

Clarity of the message: the theme which inspires the shop window and, above all, the product must be shown to be integrated within a single message that is transmitted with precision.

DETERMINING ELEMENTS IN THE COMPOSITION AND EXECUTION OF THE SHOP WINDOW

Form

Visual perception is not a passive faculty, it is an active experience in which the brain

must work on different levels. To see is to visually grasp the most outstanding features of an object, those which identify it and reveal its structural make-up in a complete and integrated schema. The factors which have a bearing on the perception of form are threefold, and act in unison: the material object, light as the medium by which the visual information reaches us, and the nervous system of the observer, which in turn will be influenced by a diversity of circumstances.

Cultural conventionalisms

As well as purely physiological conditioners, other elements also modify the perception of things, such as the experience which may have been had of an object, or the cultural conventionalisms assumed by its representation. This implies that the vision of a physical form is not a neutral act, but that it is conditioned by the personal experience which the observer, as an individual, may have had of that object, and also by his experience as a member of a society with its particular history, culture and world view.

Simplicity

A thing is simple insofar as no difficulties are presented when it comes to understanding it; the influence which is entailed in the subjective reaction of the observer, determined by cultural factors and the familiarity with which the object is contemplated, must always be taken into account. In general terms it can be stated that simplicity does not so much depend on the number of elements employed in an image, as on the structural features of that image. Simplicity is the deployment of the minimum number of elements necessary to reveal the constitution of the whole. The tenets of economy and order become the keystones in the creation of a shop window display where the criteria of simplicity prevails, economy being understood as the form of organisation of the simplest possible structure for the desired end, and order as the simplest possible manner of organising that structure.

Unity of perception

This is the result of simplicity, insofar as it dominates complexity and the synthesis of the variety of human experience. Form and meaning must correspond in order to promote precise communication; if there is a discrepancy between the two, the simplicity will be impaired and so, by extension, will the understanding of the meaning of the object or the whole.

Perspective

The tendency to mentally define forms which are only insinuated in reality. This is achieved through two mechanisms: levelling and heightening. Levelling is a process of unification, the search for symmetry, the reduction of structural features, repetition, the elimination of all that is discordant and oblique. Heightening works in the opposite direction. The result gives rise to forms which are distinct from the initial intention of the creator or transmitter and therefore gives rise to different dynamics; as the process of levelling diminishes the tension in the observer so, conversely, the process of heightening increases it.

Interaction

A fundamental aspect concerning the visual perception of form is the relation of the whole to its parts, the interaction produced between them and which tends to prevail. In general, objects are seen as a whole, and although the parts can alter the whole and vice versa this interaction is not always produced. Interactions have their origin not in the material object but in the processes of the nervous system. These interactions in the visual field are ruled by the principle of simplicity, although the rule is applied with distinct degrees of intensity, according to the conditions in which each situation is presented.

On this page, three original designs for fashion accessory shops.

On the following page, a perfumer's shop window totally dominated by the colour white, both in the flask and the foreground display, and also in the multiform structure which becomes the sole decorative element in this window display.

An example of the spatial effect of depth achieved thanks to the square flooring which is lost in the background, counterpointed by the two figures in the foreground. Conversely, below, the reduction in space forces a solution based on simplicity and suitable lighting.

On the following page, the solution adopted by a cake shop to convey to the observer a sensation of distinction and quality, through chromatic elements (the use of purple and blue), materials (objects of classical inspiration, fine fabrics) and warm and highly attractive lighting.

As a reference it can be stated that the tendency to simplify is increased in relation to the decrease in the period of observation, or due to deficiencies in the quality of the field of vision (e.g., because there is a lack of light).

There is no single definitive explanation for many of the phenomena related to this aspect, although it is known, for example, that well-organised figures preserve their integrity despite mutilations and distortions, in such a way that incomplete fragments of a figure can be perceived as the complete figure (this is the effect produced by statues such as *Winged Victory* or Myron's *Discobolus*). It appears as if the perception of a significant part of a figure by the cerebral cortex sets off a process which is capable of completing the figure in the mind, of reproducing that figure as though it were a complete perception.

Similarity and differentiation

The relation between parts was studied by the German philosopher Max Wertheimer, who postulated a series of rules including that of homogeneity or similarity. This is presented as a limited situation in which vision approaches the absence of structure; only when the composition separates similar forms does similarity act as a structural principle, due to the generation of forces of attraction between separate elements (the grouping tendency).

Grouping through similarity can respond to any visual perception (light, colour, form, etc.) and can occur both in space and in time. What must always be taken into account is that the overall composition must suggest a sufficient common base between the elements in order for perception to establish comparisons and connections which allow for grouping and differentiation.

Space

The life of man, from his very origins, has unfolded at the meeting point of two dimension: space and time. This idea was not shaped in the consciousness of mankind from the beginning, but has gradually been affirmed over an extended period of time, subject to many and diverse interpretations which have always reflected the evolutionary moment which gave them birth.

Law of differentiation

Initially applied to child development, this law, generally speaking, defines the vital space of the recently born child as an undifferentiated field (Jean Piaget). As the child grows up his space becomes increasingly differentiated because his perception and learning teach him to structure and differentiate areas which were previously inaccessible.

This principle in its most elementary form indicates that organic development always moves from the simple to the more complex. According to Herbert Spencer, differentiation also implies an evolution from the undefined to the defined, from confusion into order.

Something similar happens to the artist, both in terms of the development of his personal capacities and also in the adapting of them to his cultural and human background. The primitive artist has a lineal, one-dimensional concept of space, and forms are not specified. From this state he evolves until he develops a two-dimensional concept in the translation of reality, and from there he takes the step into three-dimensional space, where he has complete freedom.

The problem represented by contact between objects in space, and the rivalry which results from that contact, is also important in relation to the distinction between them. In lineal terms two objects which are in contact in front of an observer share a line which they dispute. This is a case not so much

On the previous page, the interaction between the different elements achieves the recreation of a certain springlike atmosphere. In the photo above, an example of an open shop window, with direct access.

Various fashion shop entrances, representing two of the basic types of shop window: in the first and fourth photos, shop windows closed in at the back, and in the second and third, windows of the shop-as-window-display type, this being the solution adopted by businesses with a generally reduced surface area, which choose not to add extra panels or doors and to convert the whole premises into a shop window displaying itself.

On this page and the following, shop windows where the use of supports and decorative elements is the key to their aesthetic look.

of superposition but of the conditional equality of the two objects.

Form and background

The most elementary two-dimensional representation is the relationship of figure and background. This is an apparently simple phenomenon, but in reality it is quite ambiguous. Theoretically the figure is placed in front of the background, but it does not always turn out to be that simple in terms of perception. The general tendency is to consider the enclosed surface as the figure and the enclosing surface as the background. This tendency presupposes that the space conceived of as the figure should be limited, and that conceived of as background should be shown as unlimited. To this affirmation can be added a complement which gives the idea of the possibilities of intervention in this sense. All enclosed figures possess a greater density than the background; this idea can be extended to include textures, and therefore by increasing the density of the texture the density of the figurative entity is increased and in this way the figurative space can be strengthened or the logical situation concerning the figure and the background inverted.

The observation that the surfaces receiving the strongest light tend to be seen as figures,

under the same conditions as the other implied surfaces, is also valid. This principle can be applied to equally saturated colours, thus, for example, red, with a tendency to advance, is more figurative than blue, which tends to withdraw.

Another factor which has a bearing on the strengthening of the character of the figure is simplicity of form and symmetry; the simplest figure will always prevail. It is useful to be aware that the convex tends to triumph over the concave, while for practical and expressive ends it is worth knowing that a convex form favours the figure and a convex form the background. This phenomenon, however, is not invariable and partly depends on where the attention of the observer is focussed.

The important thing is to perceive that the phenomenon of the figure and the background is not limited to a determined static spatial location but that, above all, it is deeply buried within a difference of dynamics. The question rests on the fact that the background, being without form, lacks its own dynamics.

The figure-background dichotomy has, however, a very limited application, as it only implies an articulation on two levels. As a rule the viewer has to confront more complex compositions, where a greater number of depth levels enter into play.

Spatial effect

The spatial effect is accentuated to the extent that man is capable of perceiving depth; when the objects in a composition are touching each other, without any interruptions, the effect will be very weak. On the other hand, the interruption of one object by another, its partial obstruction, wakes the perceptual tendency to see an overlapping, which is necessary to complete the form which is being incompletely shown.

Overlapping does not always imply hiding in an absolute sense through opacity; thus transparency can be considered as a type of overlapping when it does not encompass the whole of the background, in which case the perception which is gained does not imply overlapping.

Essential factors in transparency are light and colour. The luminosity of the area of trans-

Lights reflecting up towards the ceiling which, together with the warm colour scheme of the wall surfacing, presents a pleasant, cosy atmosphere.

parency causes effects which mix light, through addition or subtraction according to its character, and it is also one of the factors which determine which of the visual forms appears in front (there could be two or more forms).

An effect of greater depth is achieved by variations of size. This can be a very useful resource in the creation of an optical illusion which suits the anticipated goals. Obliquity is also a factor which creates depth, it being perceived as a deviation with respect to the horizontal-vertical axis, which accentuates its quality as a third dimensional relief.

Lighting

Light

Light by definition is an electromagnetic radiation, of the same nature as radio waves, which is visible to the human eye and can be thus interpreted. The natural light which we enjoy on the Earth comes from the Sun, but the perception of this reality is not evident; we appreciate the sky as being luminous in its own right and it is distinguished from the sun only in terms of the intensity of that luminosity. Something very similar occurs with objects, which are perceived as if they possessed their own light source, even though we know and we can see that they are lit by either natural or artificial light sources.

Thus, things are perceived as being luminous, which brings us to the problem of establishing the degree of luminosity of objects in order to

take greater advantage of lighting in its application to the art of window dressing. This depends, among other factors, on the distribution of the light in the available space, on the optical and physiological processes which act on the viewer, and on the physical capacity of the object to absorb or reflect the light which it receives.

Luminance and luminosity

Luminance is the property present in all surfaces which allows for the reflection of more or less light, according to the intensity of the lighting which it receives. It is important to stress that, in terms of perception, it is not possible to directly distinguish between reflective power and illumination, as only the intensity of the resulting light can be captured. The luminosity of the observed object, that is, its capacity to reflect the light, depends on the distribution of the values of luminosity within the whole of the visual field.

The creation of spaces through lighting

It is not the same thing to talk of illumination, from the physical point of view (which in window dressing would be the consideration of the lighting installation, sources, type of lamps, power, colour, etc.) as to do so in terms of perception.

Physically, an object needs to receive illumination in order to be visually perceived, although the illumination is not always seen. A three-dimensional frame illuminated by a uniform light source is perceived as if it was giving off its own luminosity. In fact this is given to the object illuminated within that frame. From a vase, for example, a scale of luminosity and colour values can be observed ranging from a degree of obscurity to a maximum point of light.

In a three-dimensional composition, such as a shop window display, the lighting and its aesthetic consequences depend on a judicious arrangement of the points of light and their distribution in the space.

An example of direct halogen spotlighting aimed at emphasising a specific element and stressing the contrast between the coldness of the metallic grey background and the pastel green of the flowers.

Another example of halogen lamp lighting; this type of lamp provides a diaphanous white light without oscillations and with a superior luminous quality.

On the right, the interior of a jeweller's shop in which a diffuse lighting has been chosen which favours the contrasts between shadow and light and softens the intensity of the colours. The diffuse lighting has been complemented by a series of spots, partly embedded in the ceiling.

The shop window of a women's fashion shop, lit at night.

Below, the interior of a men's boutique, where the light reflecting up towards the ceiling creates a warm, cosy atmosphere.

On the previous page, ambience lighting based on halogen spots.

On this page, above, an example of a shop window with an illumination based on diffuse light and, on the left, the interior of a shop where the use of classic *oeil-de-boeuf* lighting has been chosen.

The combination of colours of the different garments is the predominant note in this men's fashion shop.

On the following page, explanatory drawings of the colour circle resulting from the breaking down of white light, with the primary additive colours (red, yellow and blue) plus the fundamental and the complementary colours.

A highly valuable property of light is the creation of spaces. The strengthening of the effect of three-dimensionality provided by side lights, for example, is manifest. This allows not only for the accentuating of the volume of an object in perceptual terms but also for the accentuating of the lighting. Front lights, according to their intensity, produce effects of an increase or decrease in depth. Sharp contrasts in luminosity create effects of contrasts in distance.

Finally, attention must be drawn to an important aspect of lighting, as applied to window dressing; the dispersion of light is capable of creating a wide range of atmospheres and optical effects of great aesthetic force.

Light can either be direct or diffuse. Direct light is orientated directly on an area or a specific object, creating a strong contrast of light and shade, accentuating volumes and reliefs and with an effect which intensifies the colour.

Diffuse light presents a contrast which is less severe, softening the intensity of the colours. The choice is not exclusive, and in the same shop window, display lighting with a greater or lesser degree of diffusion can (and in fact should) be contrasted with various lighting spots which, being movable, can be directed to highlight specific aspects of the display, or products to which it is wished to give special importance.

Lighting is one of the two most important aspects of window dressing, and one of the aspects which offers the greatest possibilities for the creation of atmospheres.

Colour

Introduction to the theory of colour

Colour can be considered from many angles and its study is common to many disciplines. Colour is light and therefore its study corresponds to physics; colour is perception, and it is thus related to physiology; colour is sensation, and as such is within the field of psychology. This multi-disciplinary reality can be summed up, in practice, by saying that colour is the result of the breaking down of white light into a spectrum of colours on which the colour circle is based.

The colour circle is no more than a continuous succession of the colours of the spectrum: red, orange, yellow, green, blue, indigo and violet. Colours which are diametrically opposed in the circle, such as red and blue-green or yellow and blue, have strong contrasts, and are called complementary colours. Conversely those colours which are adjacent, such as red, orange or yellow, harmonize and create a sensation of greater balance.

The study of colours has, for many years, been centred on the idea that all colours can be obtained from a small group of fundamental or primary colours. The primary colours in the spectrum are red, yellow and blue. The secondary colours which are obtained through the combination of primary colours are orange, green and violet. By combining each primary colour with a secondary colour

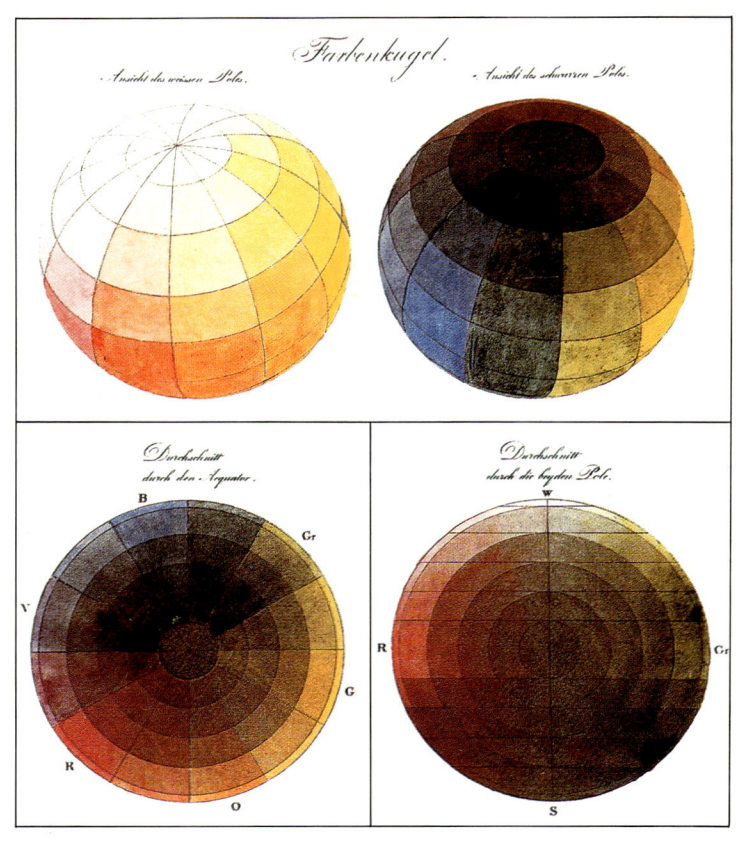

three pairs of colours are formed. In the colour circle these form a series of symmetrical pairs called complementary pairs. Yellow and violet form one of these pairs, as do red and green, blue and orange forming the third.

The skilful combination of colours allows the artist to fully exploit the language of colour and, although there is a tendency to believe in the existence of rules concerning colour combinations, colour; combinations which are definitively correct or incorrect do not exist. In all cultures and in all ages there have been conventionalisms concerning ways of combining colours; in western cultures, for example, black is the colour of mourning, a function which in India is reserved for white.

At the present time we live surrounded by colours in all aspects of our lives, not only the colours of nature, but also those provided by technology, such as the reflective colours of neon and lasers. Colours combine with and influence each other in many ways and it is necessary to be conscious of all of these different chromatic possibilities, taking from them the greatest possible aesthetic and motivational advantage.

An example of a shop window in the exterior structure of which a monochrome solution has been adopted, unifying the section of the building occupied by the shop.

On the following page, the interior of a shoe shop, where the use of colour in an absolutely original form reflects the avant-garde decor of the premises.

Colours are exposed to a great variety of circumstances which substantially modify them. One of the most influential factors is lighting, which can completely transform a colour. It is not a case of a simple transposition effect, but of what is perceived as a profound modification, given that the light colour affects the different colours of a composition in different ways.

Another factor is the perceptual interaction which is produced between colours through contrast and assimilation. If a blue rectangle is placed next to a yellow rectangle the blue rectangle will appear purplish, if the yellow is substituted for red then it will appear to be greenish. This is due to the complementary relationship: yellow completes the colour circle with purple, and red completes it with green; as blue has a tendency to both purple and green then it will reflect one or other shade, according to its circumstances. It must, therefore, be taken into account that two objects of different colours, placed side by side, can substantially modify their respective colours.

This confirms the assertion that we cannot talk of colours without taking into account

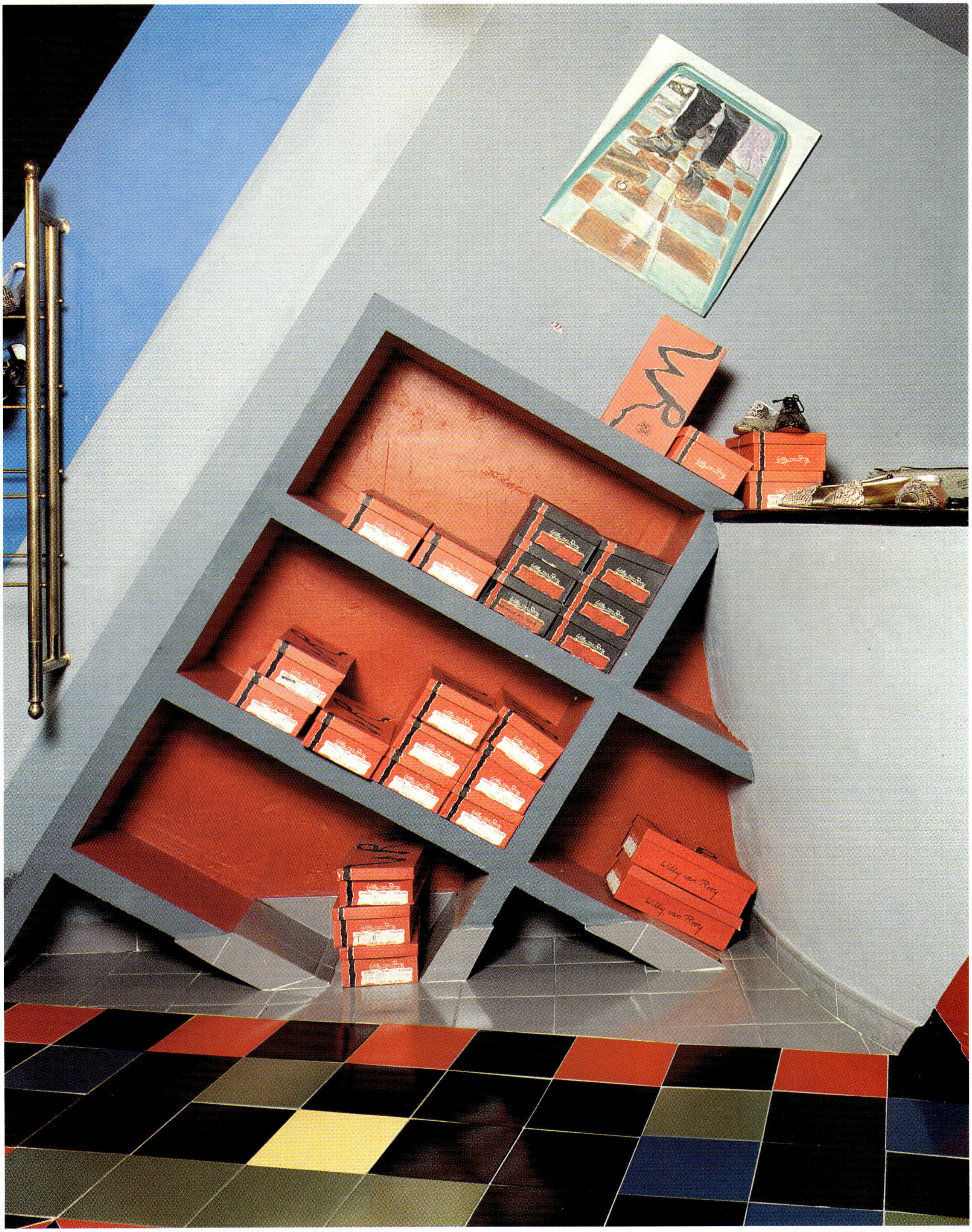
Willy van Rooy
Willy van Rooy

their context. In any well-realised composition the colours are mutually stabilised, forming a balanced and harmonious whole. On the other hand in a slapdash composition the lack of chromatic definition will be patent.

Basic dimensions: hue, saturation and brightness

In order to specify the most suitable terminology, when talking about colours, it is indispensable to define three terms referring to the basic dimensions of colour, namely, hue, saturation and brightness.

Hue is the property of the colour which gives it its name: blue, yellow, red, etc.. It is the name which is used to distinguish each of the colours in the spectrum from the others. White, black and the intermediate tones between the two are achromatic, they lack hue, as white is the sum of the reflection of all the possible colours, and black is the absence of any reflection. In order for us to perceive colour it is necessary for some of the elements which form white light to be absorbed and for some to be reflected. In this way the colour yellow is the result of the reflection of the yellow element of the spectrum and the absorbtion of the rest.

Saturation refers to the purity of a hue, in comparison with the purity that it has within the spectrum. Where it accurately recreates its

The chromatic sobriety of this Armani window display contrast with the bright colours of the Castelbajac shop, on the following page.

spectral tonality it can be said that it is highly saturated. If, on the other hand, the hue is barely recognisable, offering a neutral tonality, it can be said that it is of a low saturation.

Brightness describes the relative luminosity of a colour. White is the brightest, and black the least bright, but any colour can be lightened to the point where it is almost as bright as white, or darkened until it is almost as dark as black. Additionally, at its highest level of saturation each colour is characterised by a particular brightness, for example, yellow is brighter than violet. When the characteristic brightness of a colour is altered it loses life.

Expressivity and expression

Expression is the ultimate and indispensable condition for the success of any composition. Without expression the message is blank, the arrangement of the elements lacks clarity and the aesthetic content is incomprehensible. Visual expression can be defined as a shaping of organic and inorganic modes of behaviour as illustrated by the dynamic aspect of objects and perceptual events.

Modes of behaviour are observed and perceived in living beings as qualities inherent in themselves, being projected and perceived in inanimate objects as attributions or metaphors for themselves. But expression as a result of inorganic behaviour does not only rest in metaphorical attribution; it is also implicit in the very structure of the object and responds to the dynamics which generates that structure as a stimulus to the mental processes resulting from the perception of that stimulus.

When a man, an animal or whatsoever other object, is observed in merely physical terms it is possible that it will be perceived only in terms of size or volume... but if the attention is drawn to the dynamics of the image, then its expressive characteristics becomes evident. It is not what the eye sees, but what the mind experiences as a result of what is seen.

Expression is found in any natural process, in any arrangement of objects, in whatever daily experience, when the mind is open to the world. Expression is not a mere product of learning or of social conventionalism, although it is strongly influenced by them; it is the result of a conveniently articulated structural communication. The capacity for symbolisation of the source plays an important role in this communication: the expression of sadness is equivalent to the symbolisation of sadness in a perceptual form which is direct, primary and universal. It is a matter of manipulating composite forms to the advantage of certain perceptual schemes which intensify the expressive force of the composition and trigger off the sensitivity of the observer.

The stylist must consider and conjure with the expressive possibilities of all materials, in both the intellectual field and that of the senses. As an example, the atmosphere created by a few fabrics, some columns and a tenuous and attractive lighting effect in this footwear shop.

Simplicity is often one of the key factors which the stylist must consider in the creation of commercial spaces; a good example of this is the Stephane Kelian shop window, on the following page.

Symbolisation as an instrument of expressivity plays an important role in window dressing, as long as it is expressed through a well-conceived and structured formal scheme and based on a subject which produces a direct emotional impact.

Stylism

Stylism and the stylist

Stylism was originally understood as that literary tendency which tended to concentrate excessively on style. This term has, with time, evolved and, among other concepts, serves to define a set of formal and conceptual characteristics applicable to the world of aesthetics and fashion.

Stylism encompasses a series of standards and concepts marked by a particular use of colour, light, form, etc., and designates a way of shaping different aesthetic tendencies. The stylist is a person who is knowledgable of the formal and conceptual resources of stylism, which constitute the means by which abstract ideas are transformed and materially reflected in a real and concrete space. The window dresser and the stylist are intimately connected; theirs is the responsibility for the aesthetic and conceptual creation of the shop window display.

The stylist is the person who must combine, according to his sensitivity and intention, balance, forms, space, light, colour, movement, dynamics and expressivity. He must be a person who is open to innovation, to all the new values which emerge from society; he must be sensitive to art and must himself be a creator of forms, resources and spaces which originate from a direct experience of the world of fashion.

It is in the interests of the stylist to be receptive to socio-cultural changes, as if he were a mirror of the historical changes in his socio-cultural context and a motor for the renova-

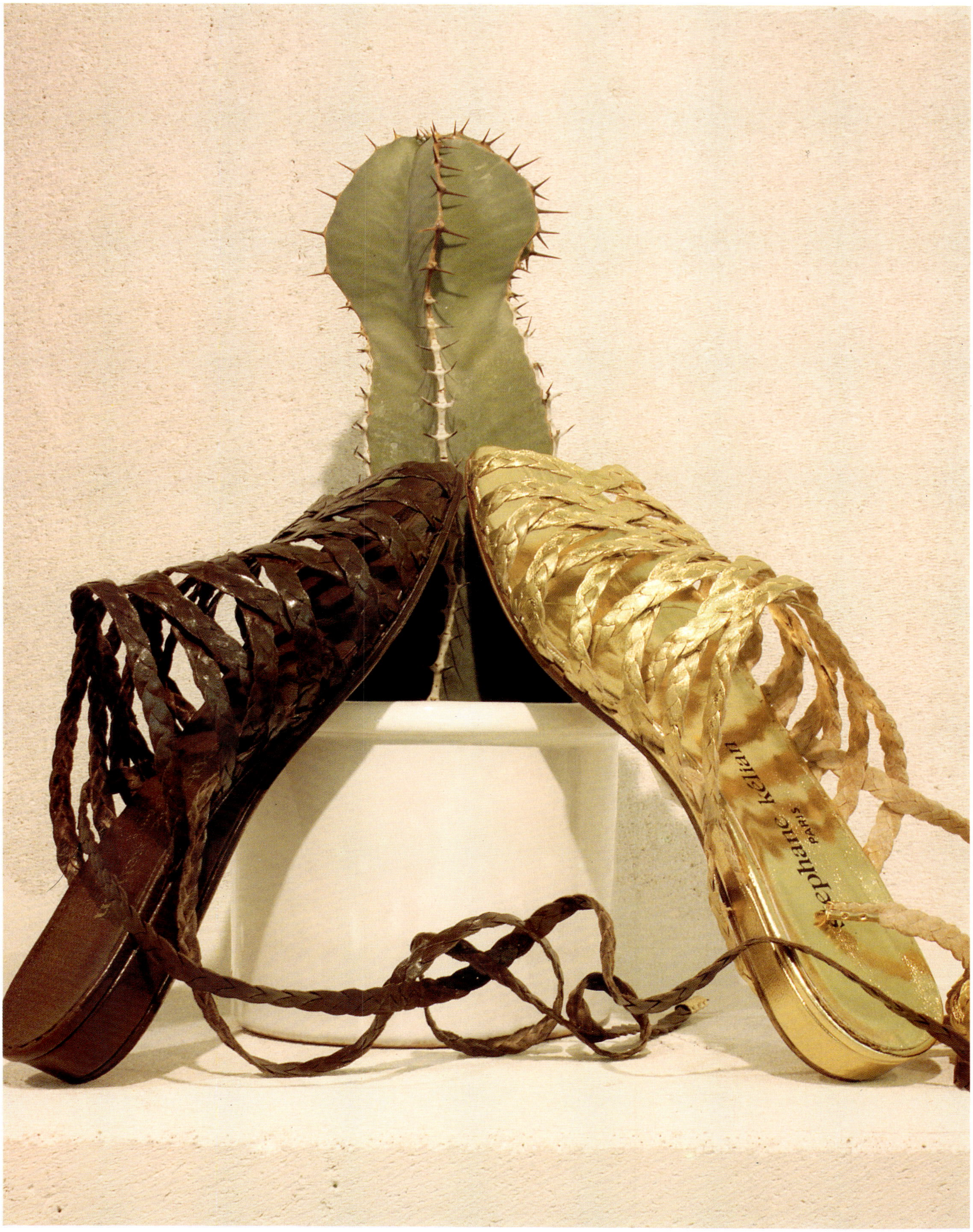
kelian
PARIS

The atmosphere recreated by the window dresser must be attuned to the kind of product being exhibited and the style required by the brand name. In the photo, elegance and sobriety are reflected in the display window of this jeweller's shop.

tion of the new aesthetics which have their influence on the man in the street. He must also pay close attention to advertising, the real pulse of our social reality, and to architecture, which forms the spaces which define our conduct, needs and sensitivities.

He has, therefore, to be a person who is sensitive to all types of cultural influences, the agent of a sensibility which is capable of transforming and transmitting in an aesthetic form the socio-cultural context in which he operates. Experiences of daily life can emerge from the culture of each individual, from that of the stylist himself, or it can have its origins in another culture or other languages whose symbolic interpretation the stylist understands and displays in this small space which he has created.

The stylist and the window dresser (although ideally they would be the same person) must be knowledgable of commercial mechanisms, of all that is related to sales techniques, marketing, motivational psychology and also of the diverse symbolisms of their age and their community. Among their qualities they must have a great capacity for organisation and planning when it comes to creating a montage. They must know the techniques and tricks of the artist and the designer, and must skilfully manipulate their tools and other material means.

On the following page, the display window of a fashion accessories shop, in which the main support, from which a soft light emanates, serves as an ideal framework for highlighting the quality of the products on display.

Style/commerce coherency

The organisation of the shop window is done in such a way that it provides information on the aims of the space, that is, it has to become a potent visual means of promotion for the premises or shop, and must not allow attention to be distracted by any other objective.

The creation of a commercial and stylistic line

An aesthetic-commercial montage offers infinite possibilities with regard to a diversity of styles and tendencies. Each creator has a style which defines the design of his spaces, yet at the same time each product, each object, each article must bring its own substance and personality to the process of creation, as a guide and a conditioner. Not only is the creative personality of the stylist important, but he must also know how to encapsulate the commercial and aesthetic objectives of the brand name and, using all the available elements, create a commercial line in shop window displays where, among other factors, the range of articles displayed, the target public, the season, the type of shop, etc. converge.

Commercial orientation

The location, the socio-economic and cultural environment in which the outlet is situated, the type of products and the aesthetic and functional nature of the space, among other elements, decide the line and the commercial orientation of the brand name.

The window dresser must decorate, distribute, arrange and illuminate, emphasising spaces and volumes, in such a way as to provide commercial and competitive solutions. The shop window, as with any other space for commercial promotion, is aimed at attracting the passer by, the potential buyer, and hold-

The shop window of a footwear shop, the access to which is through a side door hidden from the public thanks to a strategically placed plant.

ing him. Through giving a character of quality and a style, defined in terms of the commercial interests of the brand name, to this space, the passer by can be seduced, can be stimulated by the desire to enter the shop and to possess a particular article on display. In short, in that conversion of the passer by, the merely potential buyer, into an actual buyer lies the true definition of the effective commercial orientation of a shop window display.

Practical proposals for positioning

Accessibility

Access to the shop window can be from the front, the back or the side. Opting for one or the other is a decision which must be weighed up, after having taken into account a series of diverse factors:

- The shop window display space in relation to the overall space of the establishment and the access location which would be most convenient and functional.
- The opening capacity of the access in relation to its position.
- The manoeuvrability of the article through the access and the surrounding space; in some establishments, such as jeweller's, the restriction of the access to the public must be considered for reasons of security.
- The ability to work within the confines of the shop window; if the space is very narrow it may be a good idea to have a type of access which allows for one of the containing

walls to be movable, whether this be the front window itself or the back wall, by means of a sliding panel system.

Access conditions, to a certain degree, determine the possibilities of the three-dimensional space of the shop window display area; similarly, the access affects the capacity to introduce articles, ambient elements and supports, and is a key factor with regard to the ability of the window dresser to work within the space.

There are shop windows which have no back limit, and which are in direct contact with the shop. In enclosed shop windows the access door is open to a variety of solutions: an independent door, a traditional door, sliding panels, and curtains.

Composition and positioning of objects: lines, geometric forms, harmony and compositional simplicity

The composition of objects within a determined framework must follow a scheme in which the following aspects are respected: form, balance, space, light, colour, movement, dynamics and expression. On the basis of these elements the window dresser must arrange the objects with taste, variety and order.

The predominance of straight lines and compositional simplicity is one of the constants in Giorgio Armani's shops.

The display window of a jeweller's shop, access to which is through glass panels at the back, allowing the observer a view of the interior of the shop.

On the following page, an example of an open access from the interior of the shop. The harmonious arrangement of the objects and the use of neutral colours for the product stands produces a sensation of compositional balance and serenity.

The structural element *par excellence* is the line in its different configurations: straight, curved, wavy, broken, etc.. Lines delimit contours, insinuate figures, divide spaces and express sensations such as movement, stillness or repose. There is a psychology of lines, which emerges out of the fact that different lines produce particular sensations in the mind of the observer; diagonal lines emphasise action, and curves and spirals, movement; vertical lines give a sensation of height, producing an effect of dignity and elevation; horizontal lines suggest serenity and balance; and, among many other interpretations, radial lines emerging from a central hub inspire light and hope.

Lines can be structured in basic geometrical forms, such as squares, rectangles, circles, ovals and triangles, each of which has a characteristic language and a specific expressive capacity.

Harmony is fundamental in all compositions: each object must be granted an established order, related to its form and size. For example, large objects should be placed together, as long as they respond to the same functional criteria, and small objects should be used as a contrast in order to create variety within the whole. Harmony is the balance of forms, sizes, colours and textures, and a key element in the success of any shop window display.

Harmony is generally based on compositional simplicity, that is, the elimination of all superfluous elements from the general discourse of the shop window display, until only those elements which are indispensable remain, and which, arranged in a balanced manner, attract the attention of the observer, which is the final objective of all shop window displays.

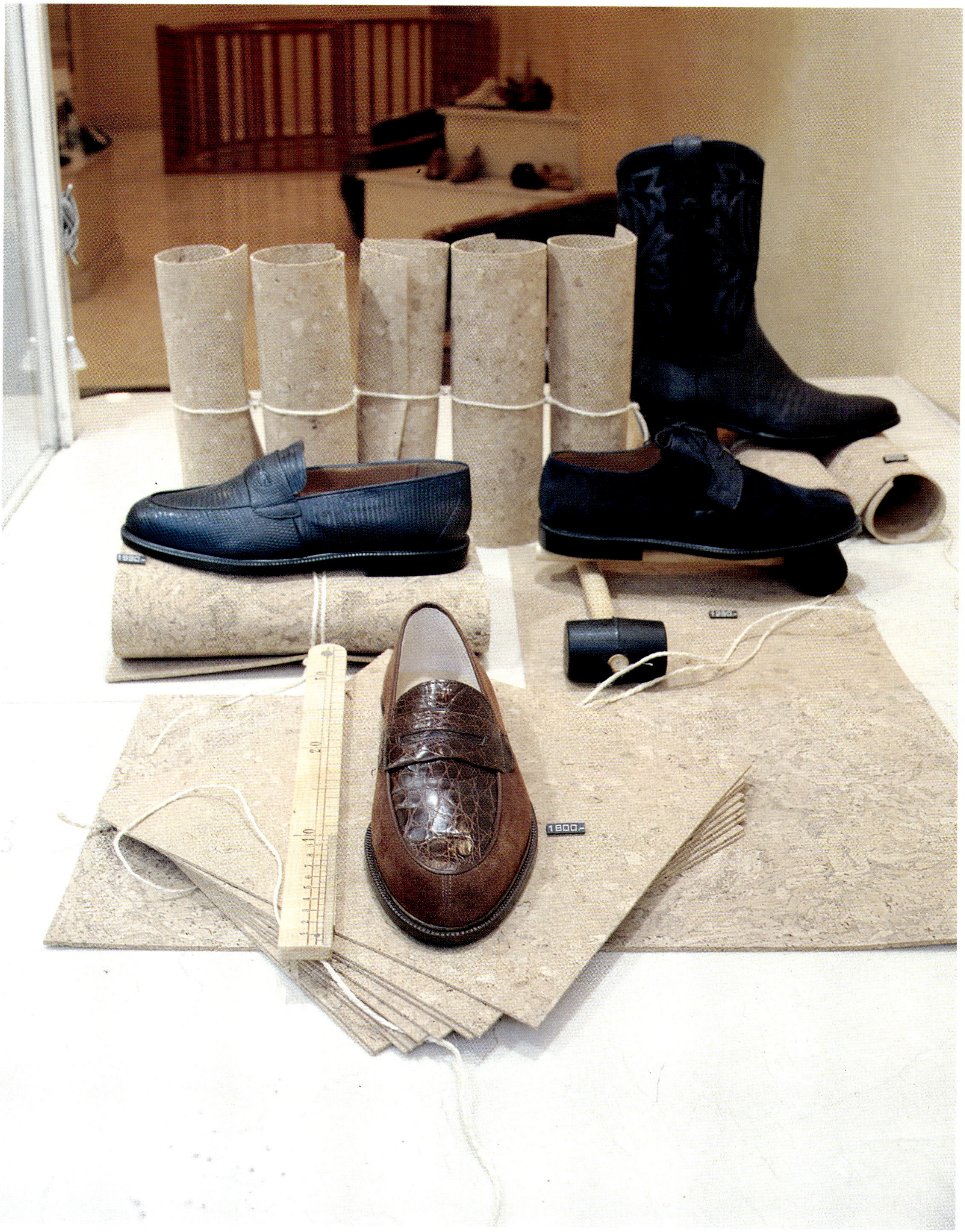
1800.-

BYBLOS

Giorgio Longoni

A view of the interior of the shop, with the staircase descending to the lower level. The commercial style of Byblos is essentially expository, giving the same importance to the exterior window dressing as to the interior display.

On the following page, above, an illustration of the considerable size of the exterior shop windows; their accessibility from the interior is direct at certain points, and at others through separating partitions.

This fashion shop in the centre of Milan is designed in such a way as to grant primacy to those spaces set aside for display. In fact the commercial aim of Byblos is that window dressing should be the principal offer to their customers. The premises constitute an area from which to observe and choose, the owners, in this way, seeking to enhance the pleasure of going shopping.

Due to the formal characteristics of the premises, which occupy the greater part of the façade of the building in which they are located, windows of a large size were viable, without any visual interference, and framed by simple metallic blue structures. The available space behind the windows extending, as it does, into the sales area itself gives rise to the creation of veritably scenographic installations which constitute the perfect framework for the collections which are on display.

The exterior window dressing is based on the positioning of mannequins, which give a reciprocal continuity through their postures, and rounded wooden modules which run through the window display area and which are used to seat some of the mannequins. The

Below, a view of the two mannequins, the only protagonists of the window dressing, in which a criterion of simplicity and purity reigns.

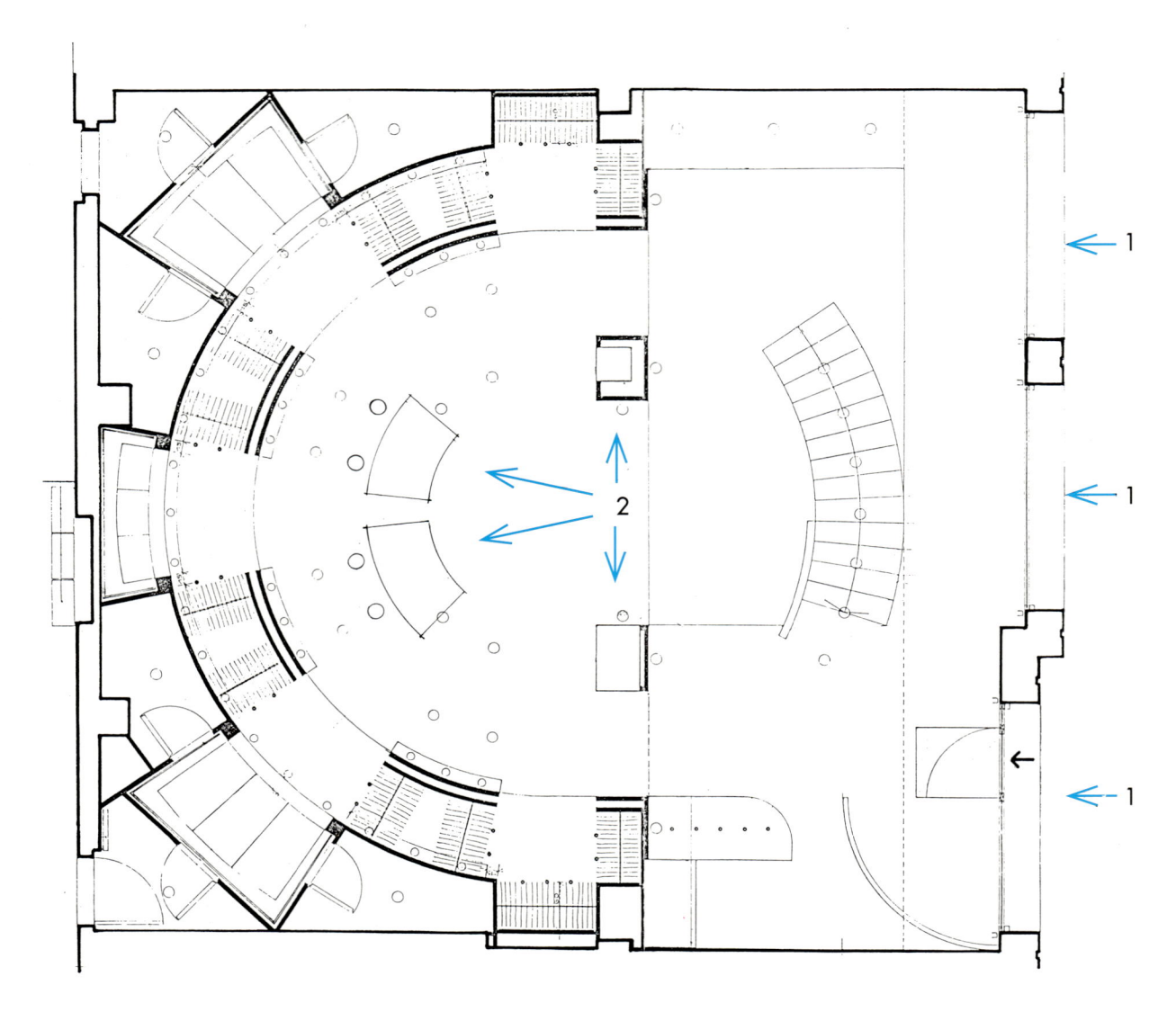

disposition of the windows in enormous frames offers a completely open perspective of the interior area, extending the display beyond the shop window as such. Within the shop a series of counters are arranged, serving as display areas for the garments, and harmoniously reflecting the curved structures of the walls.

All of this is integrated into a balanced whole in which the shop window and the interior merge, offering the observer the suggestive image which the Byblos brand name wishes to transmit.

A plan of the premises, in which, on the one hand, the window dressing area itself (1) is indicated, and on the other, the area of the shop reserved for internal display (2).

On the following page, a view of the shop window from the interior, showing, in the foreground, the rounded display counters and, in the background, the large shop windows display area. The scenographic character of the whole composition is emphasised by the consistent use of light, decorative tones and an illumination based on direct and indirect lighting spots which create a variety of atmospheres.

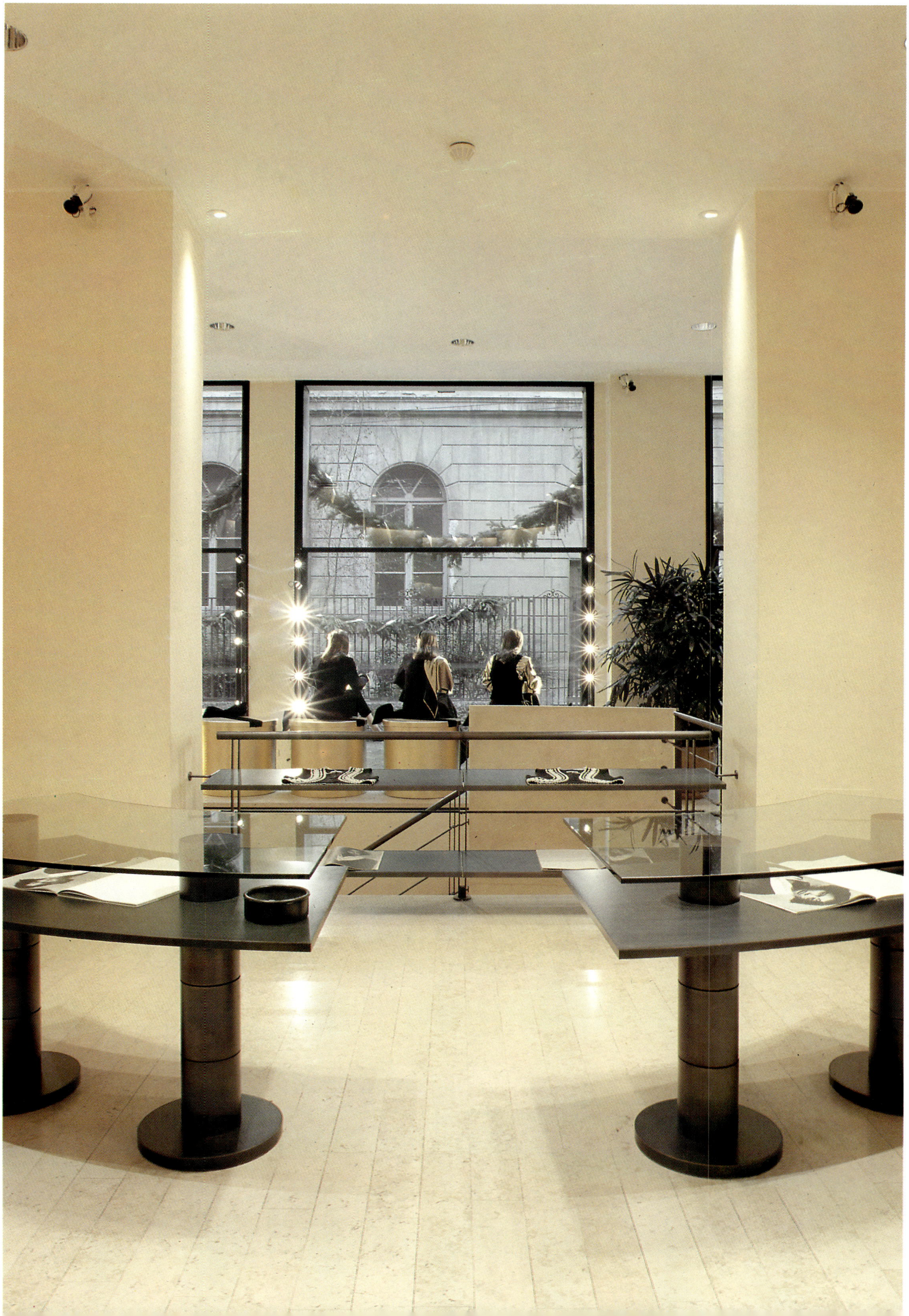

JIGSAW

Nigel Coates (Branson Coates Architecture)

A view of the shop from the interior, with the entrance doorway on the right and, on the left, the main shop window.

On the following page, an illustration of the decorative style used in the shop windows. The use of vegetation, as well as being a means of decoration, contributes to the establishment of a scenography which is aimed at creating an ideal framework for the transmitting of the Jigsaw style.

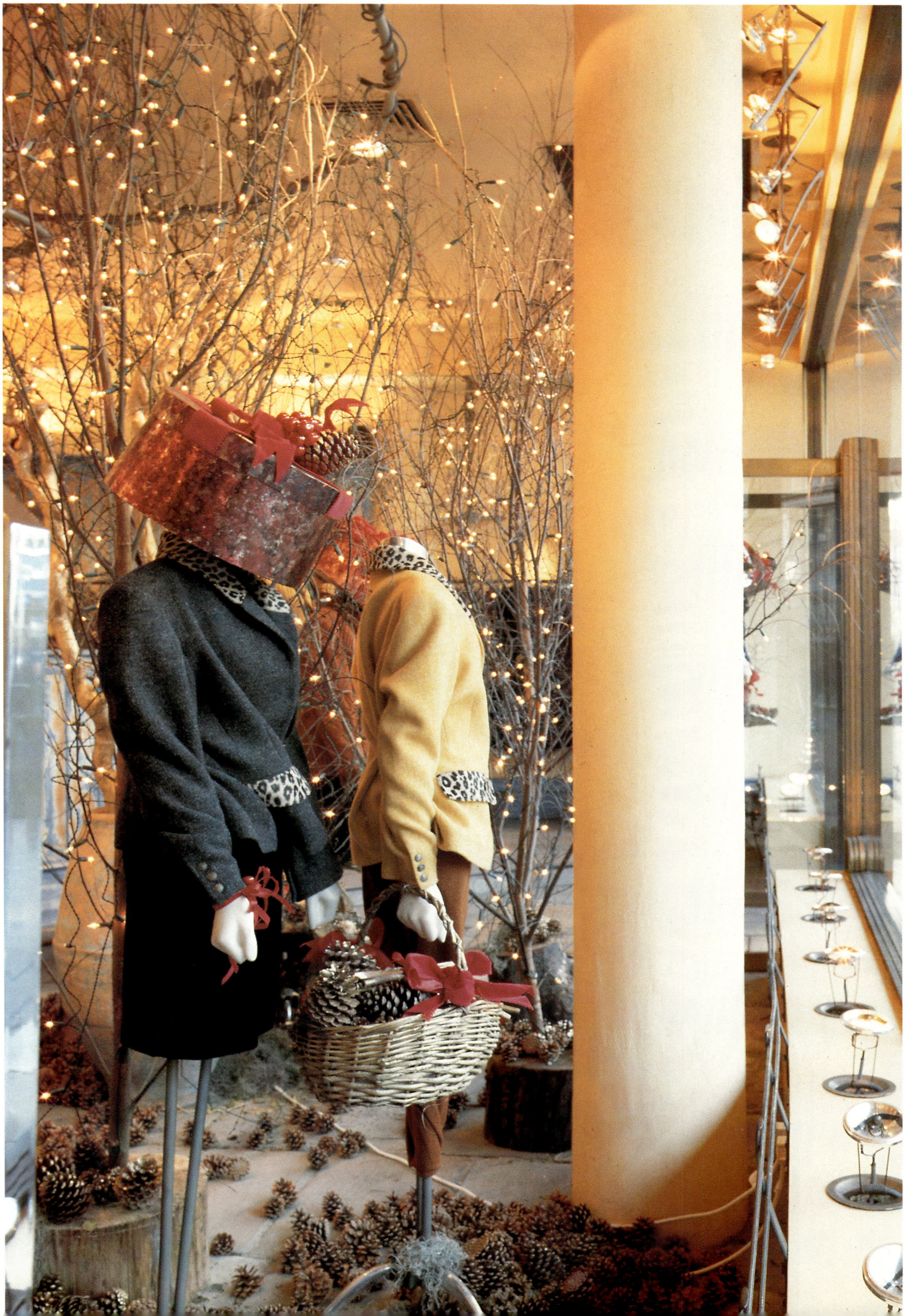

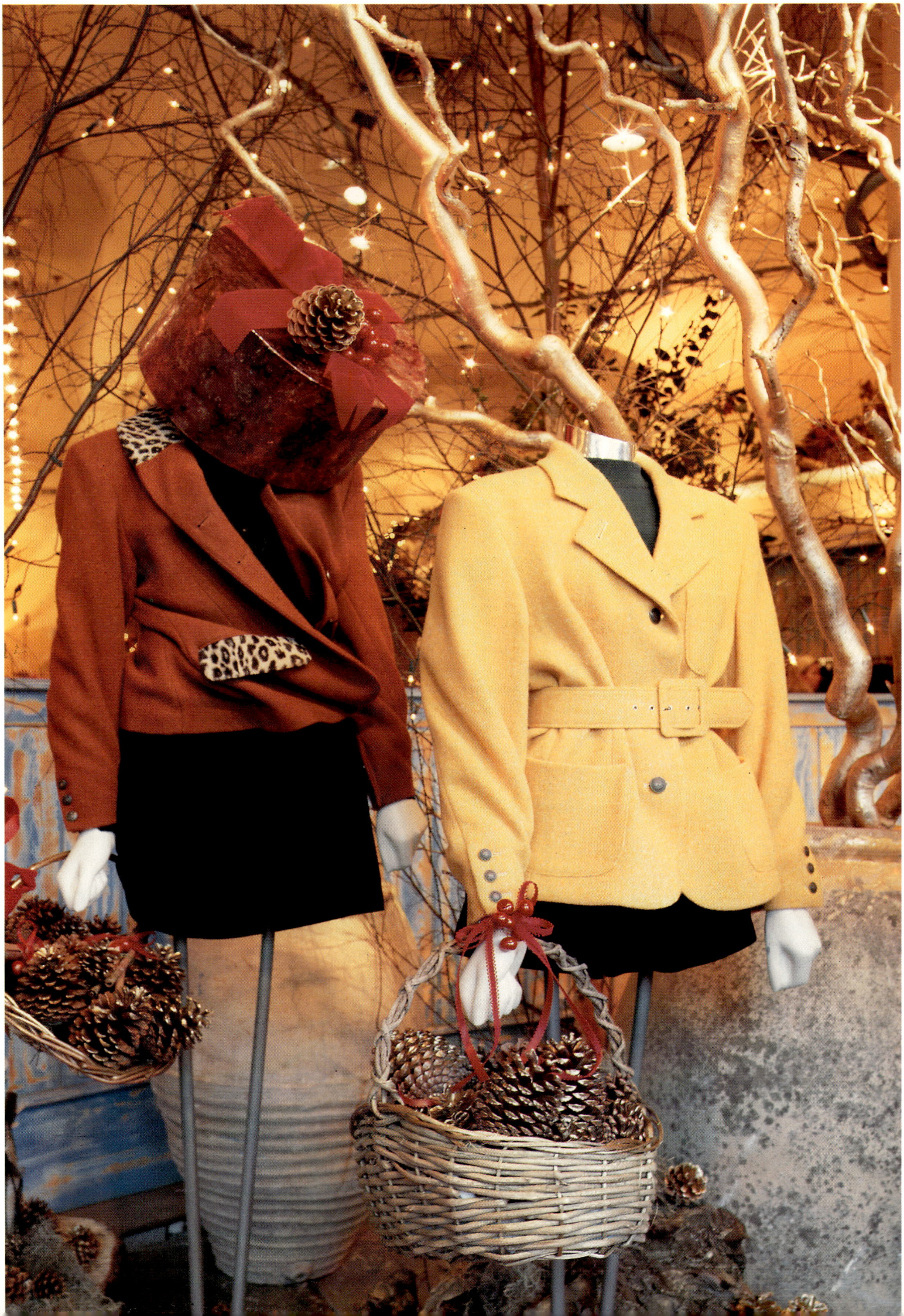

On this page and the previous page, different views of the shop window, from both the exterior and the interior. The wooden partition, which is also used as a support for the clothes hangers and as a decorative element for the shop interior, is visible through the shop window.

Nigel Coates, of the Branson Coates Architecture studio, has played his cards on an original sense of movement, as against the traditional sense of static detail, in his design of Jigsaw, achieving a fluid and, above all, theatrical sense of space.

The display areas are separated from the rest of the premises by panels which gradually converge. The combination of colours and the use of plants leads to the creation of a cheerful and pastoral atmosphere, constituting a scenography which provides a context for the garments and which manages to transmit a conclusive message in terms of the commercial image of Jigsaw.

The clothes supports are three-dimensional aluminium mannequins, an important aspect in the giving of form to the garments. The colours used have been selected in perfect consonance with the atmosphere created, offering a wide autumnal range. Weathered wooden panels separate the shop window properly speaking from the rest of the shop, at the same time creating a sweeping movement in the interior. Two rows of directional halogen spots, located at the top and at the bottom of the main window, spotlight the various garments and complement the effect of the indirect interior light, reflected up towards the ceiling, and of the diminutive light points distributed among the decorative vegetation. This type of lighting creates an attractive and pleasant atmosphere which contributes to the endowment of a peculiar and original style to Jigsaw, a personality which distances it from the more typically British shops.

ADRIANA MODE

Gigi Bolzoni & Vanna Brega

A view of the façade of the shop, with the window area and the entrance doorway framed by large, dark stone blocks.

On the following page, below, a floor distribution plan of the premises, with the shop window area indicated by arrows.

A view of the interior of the shop. The trademark appears on the entrance door, which is flanked by two windows separated from the interior by adjustable cloth curtains.

On the following pages, a decorative mannequin inside the shop, and a view of one of the smaller shop windows, with the decorative constant provided by the plants and the chromatic unity which predominates in all of the shop's stylistic compositions. The horizontal bar from which the coat hangs is a good expressive means for the creation of an illusion of spatial perspective.

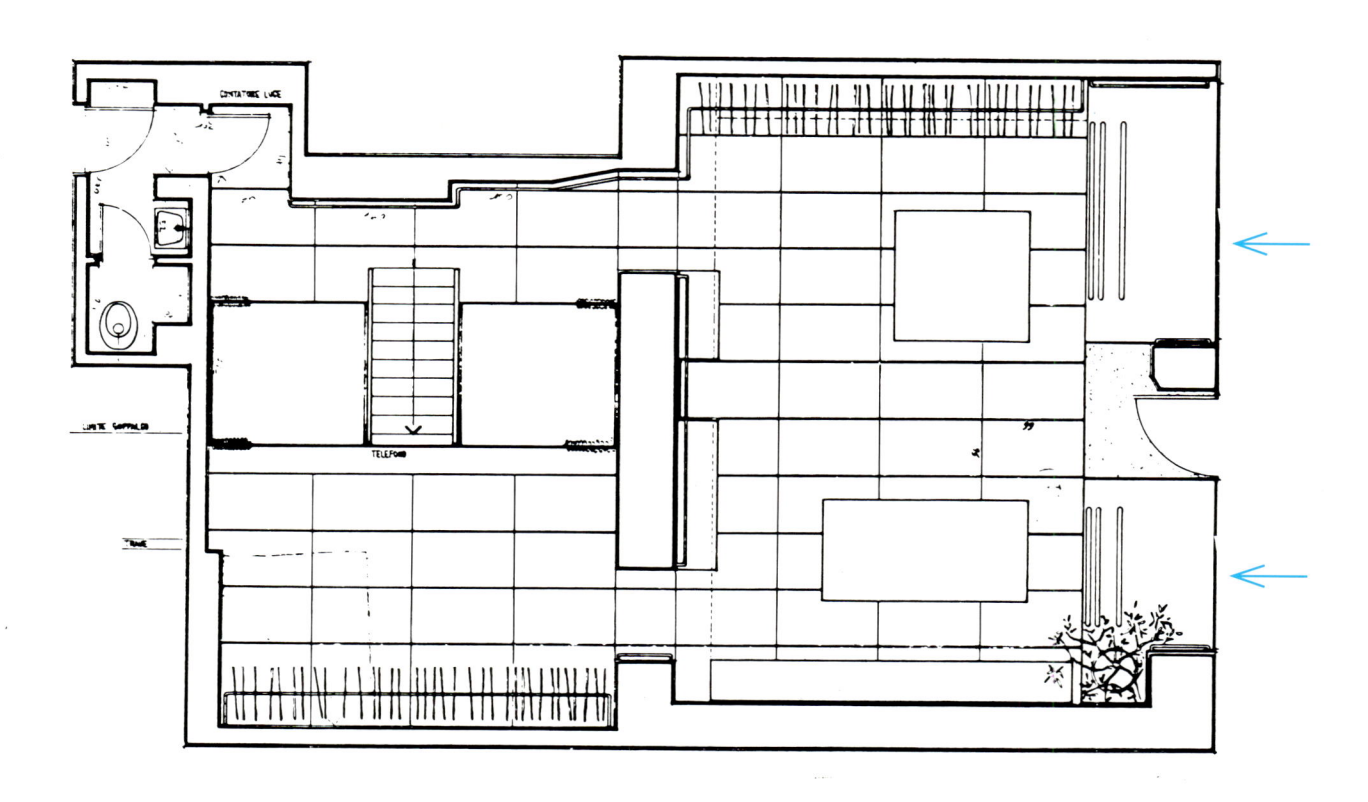

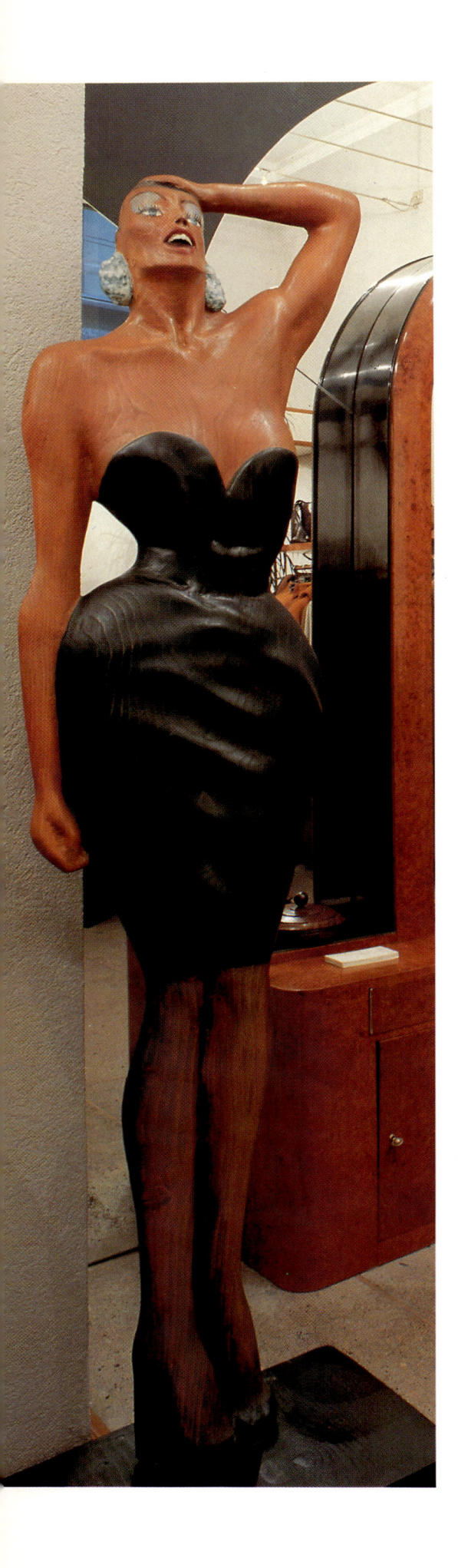

The women's boutique Adriana Mode is located in old refurbished premises, perfectly adapted to the commercial demands and criteria of the latest fashion tendencies. Three street-level shop windows, of a relatively small size, display the material. A mannequin is seated beside some horizontal wooden bars, on which clothes and complementary accessories are displayed, achieving a sensation of ease and informality. The mannequin is fully dressed, sporting the more basic articles and also a coat and complementary accessories.

The space in each window is fully taken advantage of to show a wide range of clothes and complementary articles which reflect the commercial spirit of the owner, distancing the shop from any elitist interpretation it might be given. Great care is taken over the combination of colours and tonalities of the models on display. Plants are used as a decorative element which, as well as granting a compositional balance, also contribute to the creation of a relaxed atmosphere.

The lighting solution which has been adopted is suited to the small size of the premises, providing a uniform atmospheric lighting effect, complemented by small halogen lamps in the interior.

The accessibility of the shop windows is in some cases direct and in others through the height-adjustable cloth partitions. The garments in the window display are placed on a granite platform.

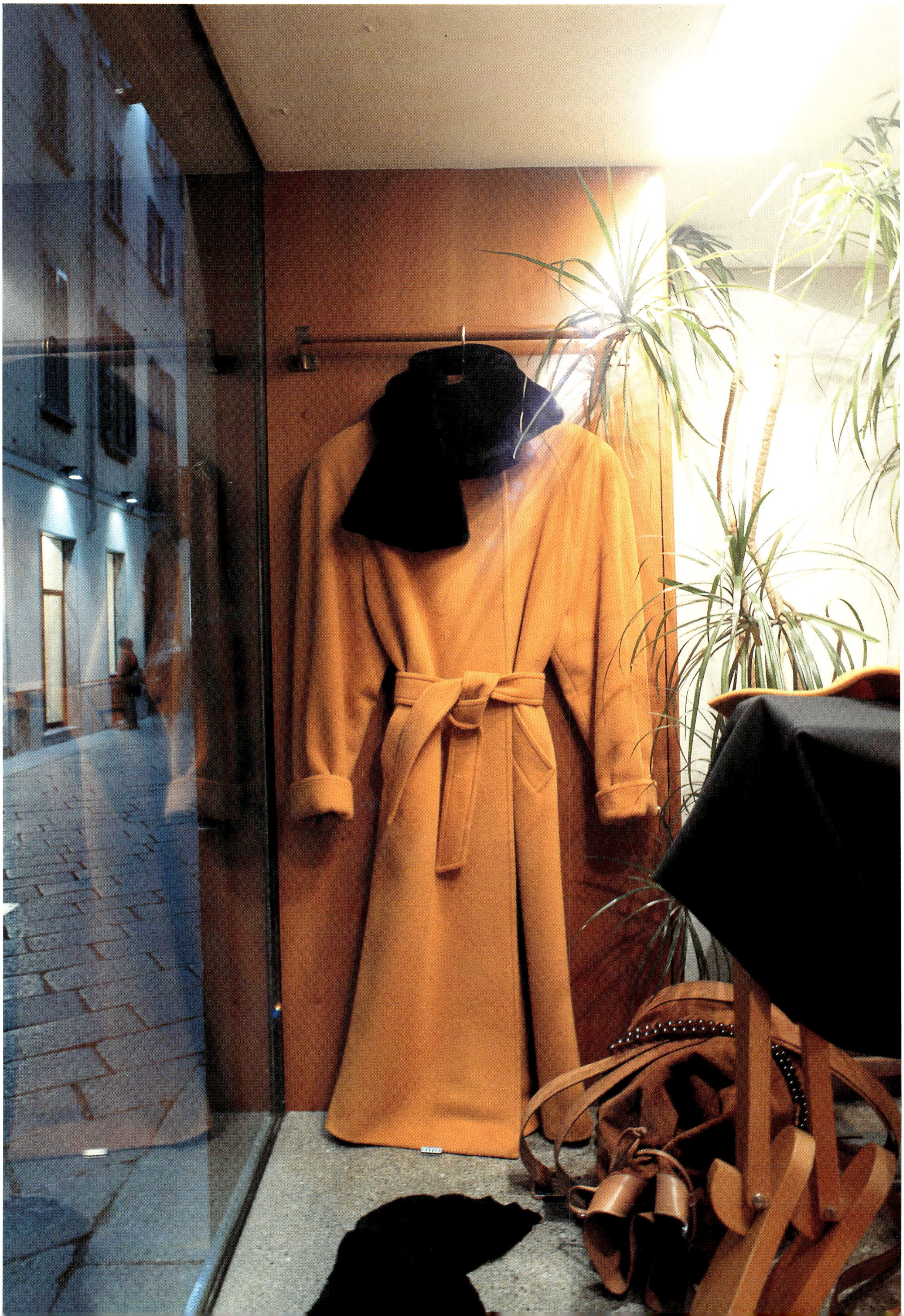

LOEWE

Itziar Esteban-Infantes & Gustavo Torner

The main window, in which the curvaceous wooden structure which supports the various fashion accessories catches the eye. Warm tones are predominant, flattered by attractive lighting based on indirect halogen spots.

On the following page, below, detail of various Loewe products, displayed on the original wooden support which constitutes the protagonist in the decoration of the shop window display.

Shots of the mannequins, which adopt dynamic postures, giving life to the garments they wear.

In this shop the creation of a scenic background has been staged which shows off the clothing articles and accessories, their beauty, quality and appeal, to the best advantage through the creation of an ideal atmosphere where the balance between the public and the private has been finely judged, allowing every visitor to appreciate and enjoy the articles which are on display.

The woman who wears Loewe has an image of elegance and seduction, subtlety and femininity, and the intention is the expression of this image through the company's decor and window dressing. The mannequins, for example, have a figurative form, allowing the postures to be chosen to suit a variety of combinations and occasions. A certain sense of movement has been created in the different scenes, an interrelation between customer and product, partly aimed at the evaluation of an important aspect of the Loewe collections: the leather articles which are the cornerstone of the company.

The purpose of the window dressing is the selling of a complete idea, the idea of Loewe. Not just a bag, or a perfume or a coat but a whole style. The different shop windows have also been designed with the aim of displaying all the beauty of the garments, of creating a warm and seductive framework which is attractive and invites you to enter and look around.

The classical lines, with the avant-garde styling of their design, identify the image of the brand name of this universal Spanish company that is Loewe.

On the left, a view of two of the mannequins, entirely dressed with the company's clothes and complementary accessories, from shoes to sunglasses.

On the following page, view of the shop window, seen from the interior and constituting a framework of great plastic beauty, transmitting the company's own sense of class and style to the customers.

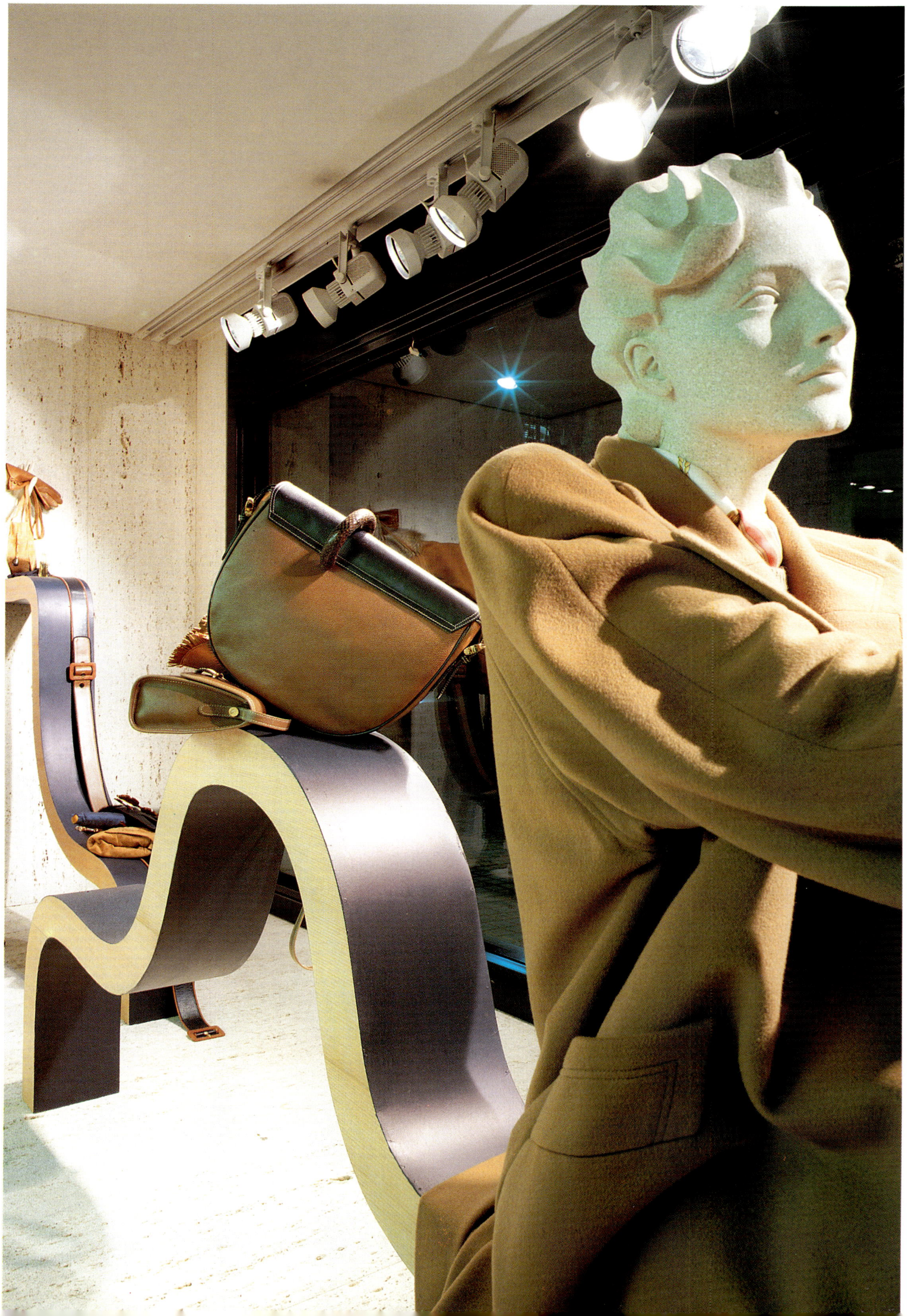

LOJA DAS MEIAS

Carlos Tojal (T&T Arquitectos)

A view of the side of the window display next to the entrance door. The backdrop consists of the same brick walls which appear inside. The base of the display window is triangular, the background consisting of two basic planes, on the left, the brick wall mentioned above, and on the right, an opening into the shop. The intersection between the two planes is hidden by a white screen which reflects the light.

Loja das Meias is an establishment dedicated to clothes, accessories and perfumery for women, situated in a modern shopping mall in the centre of Lisbon. It has a large L-shaped shop window which allows an exhaustive display of goods. On the short side of the L, which is also where the entrance to the interior of the shop is located, the painted brick walls act as the backdrop. On the longer side, what appears from the exterior to be a folding screen is in fact the back of the bag display counter.

Throughout the display window area of the shop mannequins are distributed in different postures which serve as reference points for a composition of articles representative of the complete range of products available inside the shop.

The shop window is lit by powerful spotlights attached to a steel structure, which create a combination of direct and indirect light. The central spot projects onto the back screen, creating two areas in the window: the vertical group (of mannequins), and the horizontal (of complementary accessories). The powerfully lit screen makes the mannequins stand out in contrast, backlighting the whole and accentuating the volumes.

A side window, with the mannequins as the centre of a composition of articles.

The size of the premises allowed for the location of raised circular daises, where mannequins are displayed alongside a selection of articles.

On the following page, a view of the main window display, with two of the mannequins and a rich variety of complementary accessories arranged on the dais in the shop window.

Different views of the shop's window displays, both from the interior and the exterior.

Inside, the size of the premises allows for the strategic location of circular daises where various mannequins are arranged, accompanied by decorative objects and a sample of the variety of articles which are for sale in the establishment. Glass show cases and lacquered wooden counters impose an individual style on the accessories sales area; the back of the glass show cases containing the bags serves as the background to one of the window displays.

ESTÉE
ESTÉE LAUDER
PERFECT
LIPSTICK
BEST-SELLING FRAGRANC
BEVERLY HILLS.

TRAU

Estudio de Diseño y Decoración G.C.A.

The shop window with four mannequins as protagonists and supports for the garments on display. The combination of wood, glass and steel and the precise lighting create a whole which projects a highly attractive image.

On the following page, a view of the window from the interior of the shop, where sobriety and classicism predominate. Access to the window display is direct, there being no separation between the display and the rest of the shop space (they even share the same wooden parquet flooring).

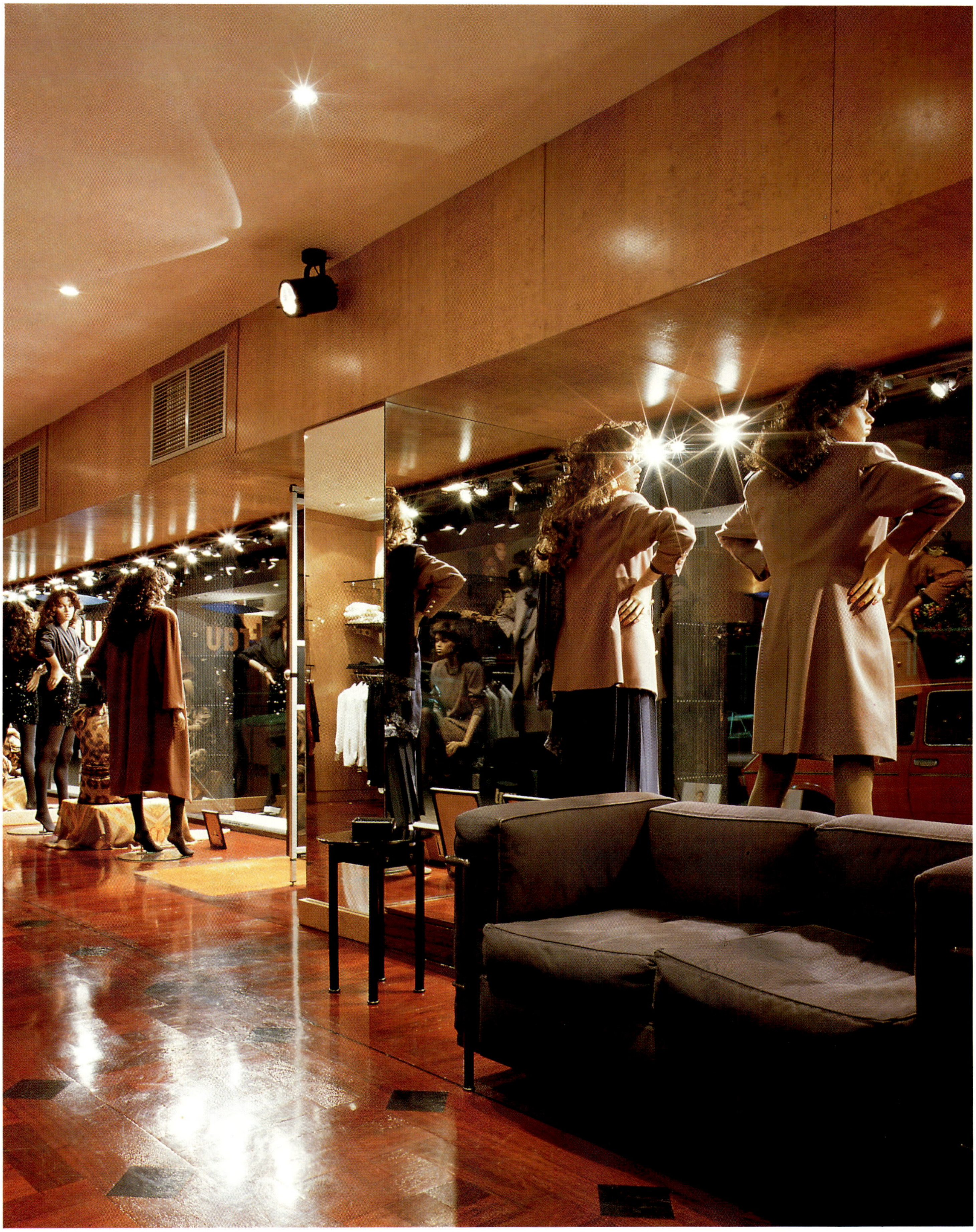

Above, a partial view of the shop window; in the upper area the strip of directional spots which illuminate the window. The built-in halogen lamps are also visible in the interior.

Below, an interior distribution floor plan of the shop with the window display area indicated by the arrows.

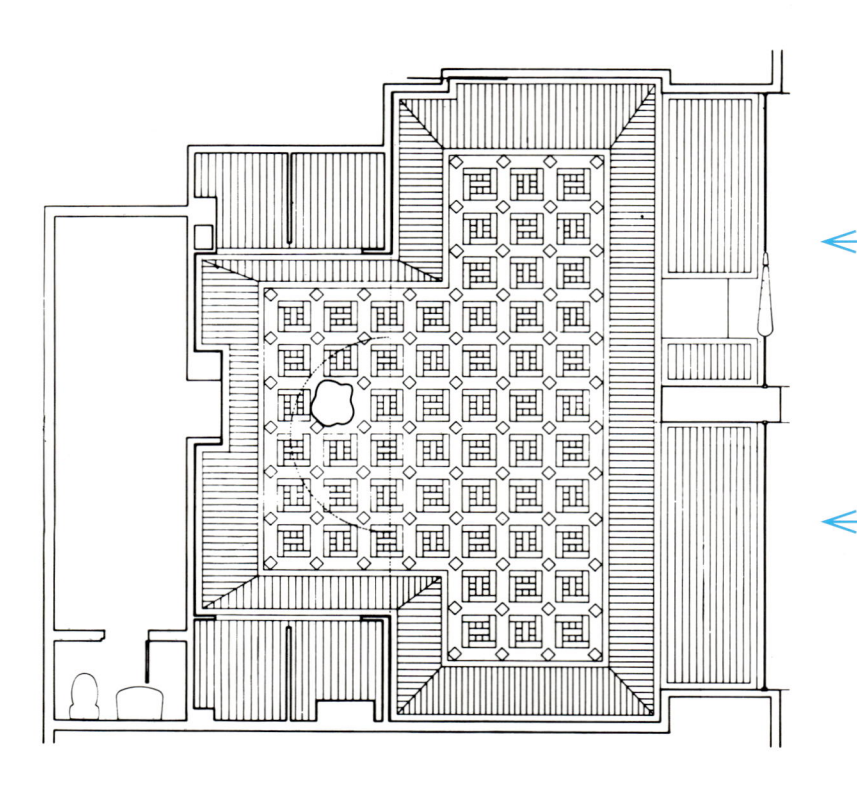

Access to the establishment is gained through a glass door; the entrance lighting is installed in the upper part, clearly illuminating the company's trademark. It presents an attractive diorama in that the combination of image, light and colour is seductive and offers an open invitation to stop and enter.

The idea was to create a warm, traditional image, through the shop window and the interior, which would draw the passer by into the interior of the shop. The shop window display is rectangular, open at the back, and with the same parquet flooring as the sales area.

The composition is based on a symmetrical balance, with one of the mannequins slightly to the left of an imaginary line drawn through the centre, a simple composition articulated

Different views of the Trau shop window display. In the photo below the company's trademark is visible, screen printed onto one of the strategically placed mirrors at the side, giving a greater sensation of space.

around three main elements, the three mannequins, with scarcely any atmospheric complements.

The dynamics are supplied by the lines of vision of the mannequins which create a sensation of direction. The central mannequin and the one on the left return the gaze of the observer, while the mannequin on the right looks directly at the mannequin on the left, forcing the eye to return once again to the overall disposition; this makes it obvious that the shop window is to be read from left to right, and having got to the right the observer finds his eye thrown back to the left again, thus having to make a second reading of the compositional whole.

The lighting is based on built-in halogen lamps in the interior and spot rails in the shop windows, contributing to the creation of a warm, attractive atmosphere which brings out the beauty of the garments. The clothes are always at the forefront of fashion, shaping the personality of Trau and defining it as one of Barcelona's most prestigious boutiques.

ANA SALAZAR

Ana Salazar

Front view of the shop window display. The harmonic composition is emphasised by the balance of the lines, the suitability of the colour combination and the simplicity of its elements, prominence only being afforded to that which is of real interest, with no superfluous or unnecessary display accessories.

Next page: a view from inside the shop, with the mannequin dressed in an original and amusing model in red and orange tones by Ana Salazar.

73

A detail of one of the mannequins and a view of the façade of the shop, both at night and during the day; in the former case the lighting is supplied by four large black spots located at the top of the shop window.

On the following page, the trade name in large silver letters written over the low black unit for displaying various models of shoes.

The façade of the Ana Salazar shop, conceived by the designer herself, consists of a large window divided in two by a narrow column, which reaches from the floor to the ceiling. To the left of the column mannequins have been arranged dressed in models from the autumn-winter collection.

In the upper part of the window display the name of the designer appears on a base of Portuguese granite in mottled black, grey and white tones, the same material which has been used for the general decoration of the shop. The shop window is intimately integrated into the body of the shop, forming a structural whole, with the same granite flooring, walls and columns. The composition presents an almost perfect symmetrical balance.

These are wide and spacious premises, completely visible from the exterior; in this sense it can be considered as an example of the shop as display window. Towards the front there is a low black display table with silver legs, on which various models of shoes are arranged. A rail, also in silver, follows the line of the display counter and is adorned with a collection of belts which hang from it.

The flooring throughout the premises is paved in Portuguese granite in black, grey and white tones, the same material being used for the walls.

Alongside the two mannequins in the shop window there are some original and modern shelving units, in the form of a pyramid, on which a few jerseys are draped.

The lighting for the whole premises is based on the use of large halogen projectors.

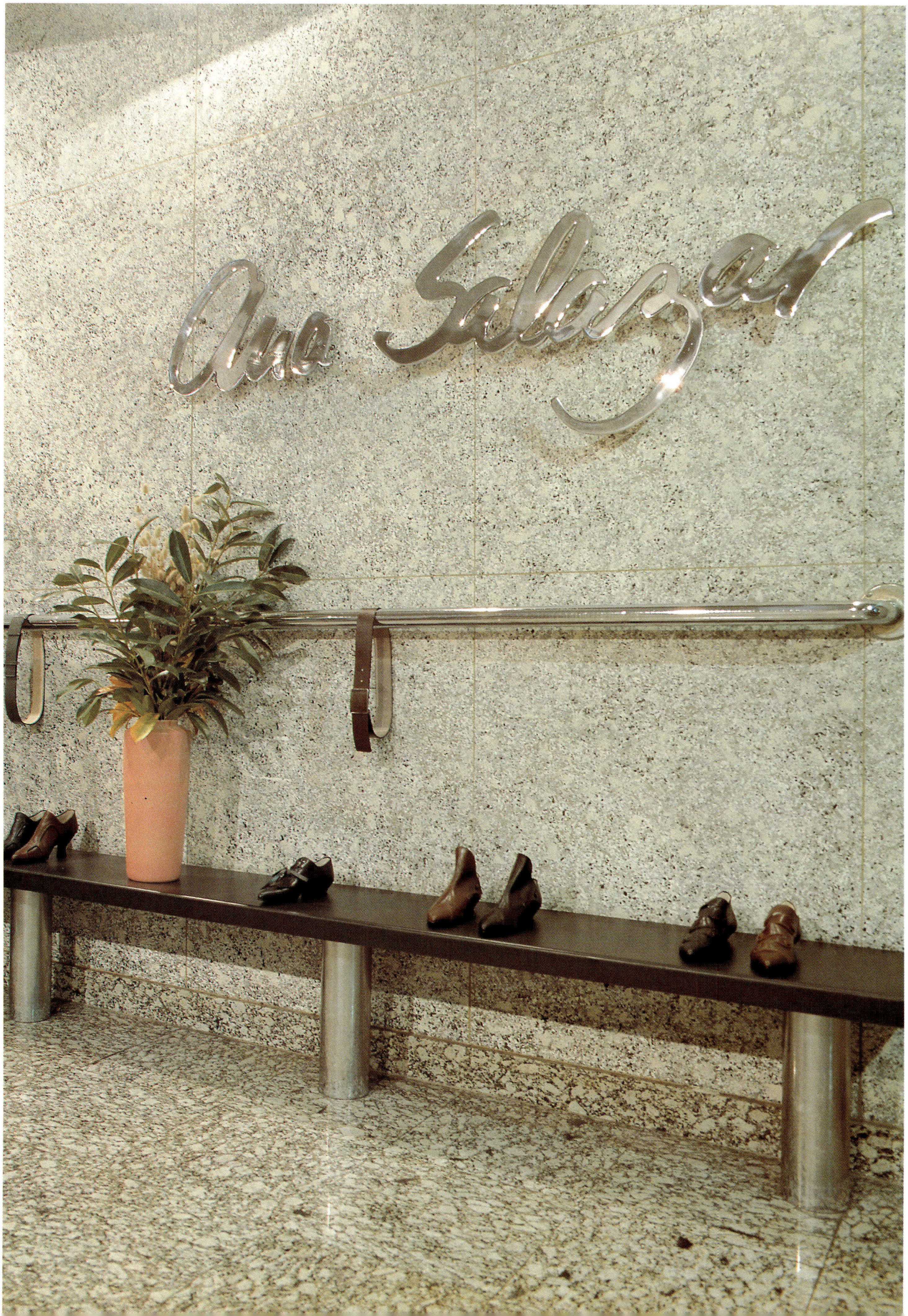
Ana Salazar

ESPRIT

Treitl & Steffel (Sottsass Associati)

A group of illuminated display cases placed in the central aisle. As with the exterior shop windows, some of the mannequins are placed on raised platforms, while others are at floor level.

On the following page, a view of the access to the shop, which is gained by crossing a bridge spanning the distance between the original and the new façades. The large, modern shop window displays contain mannequins with several models in bright colours contrasted against a white background.

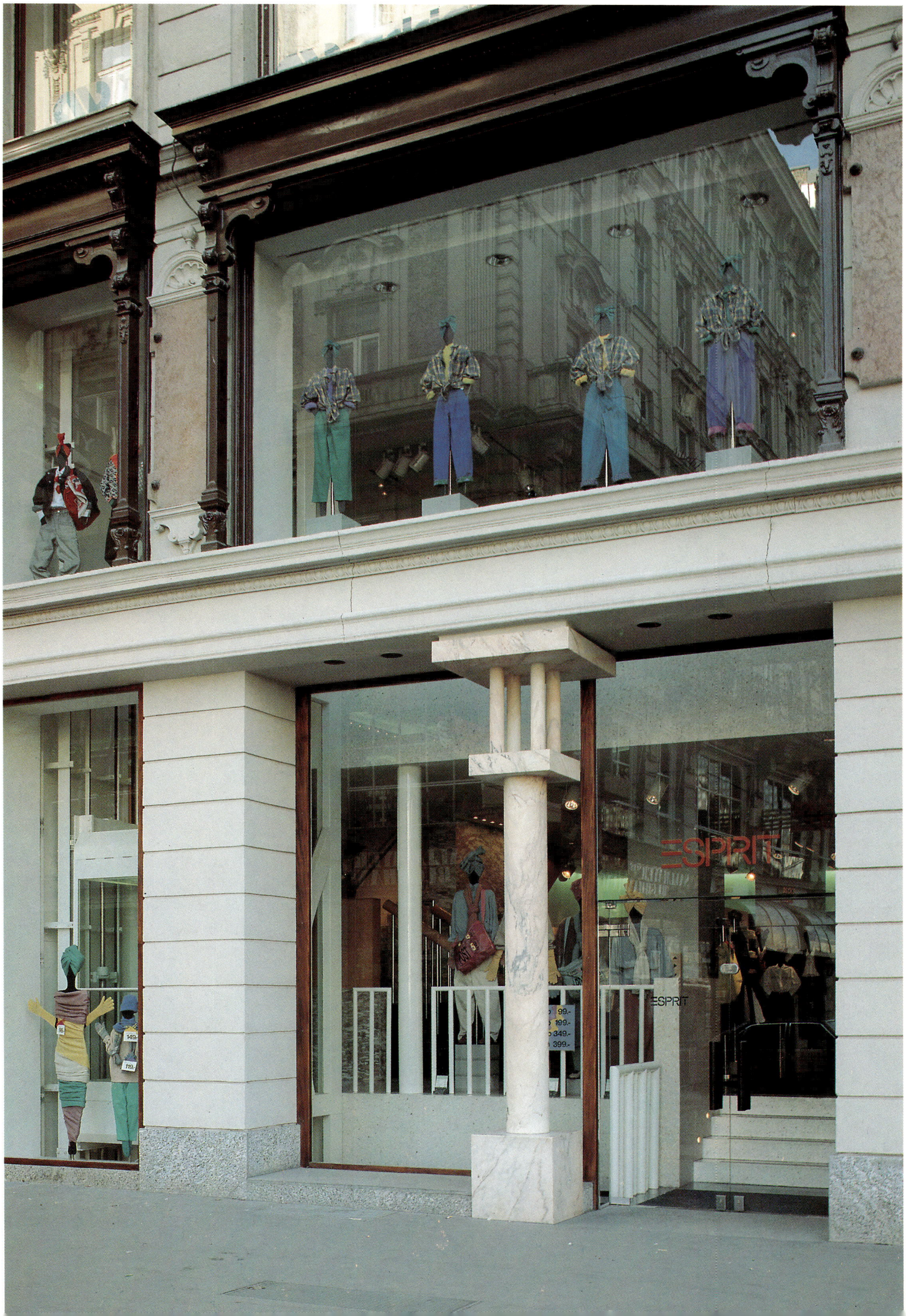
ESPRIT

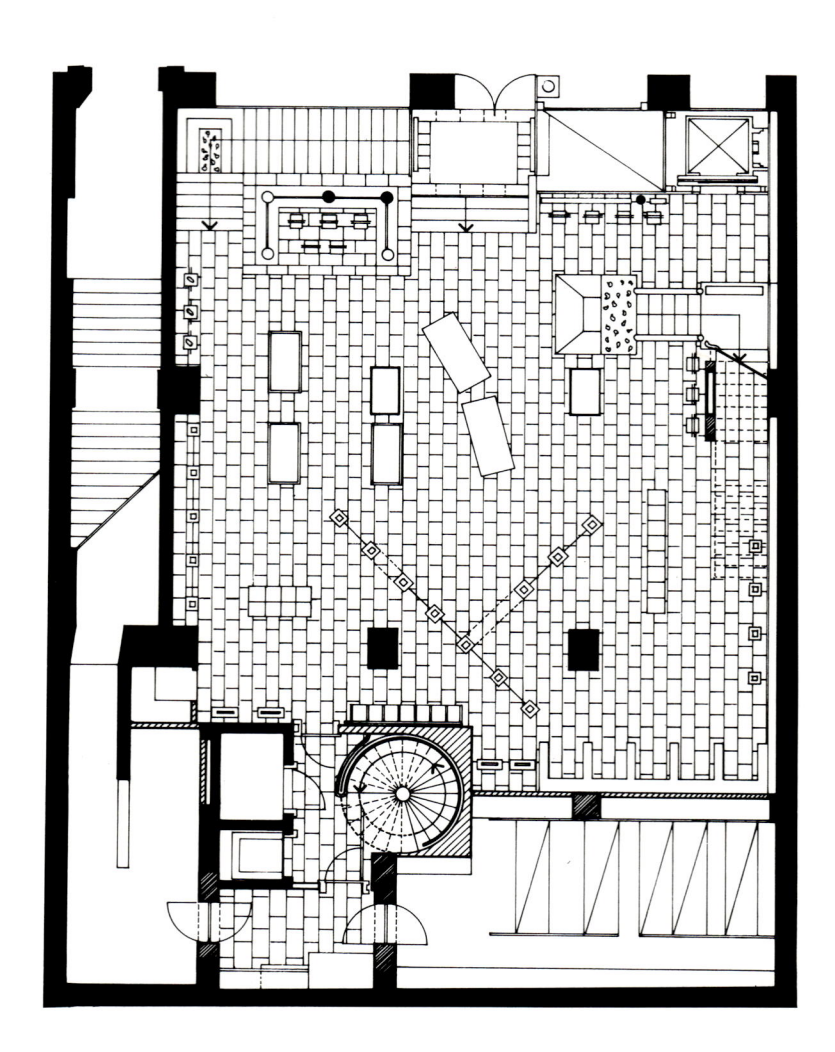

The Esprit shop occupies an XVIII-century aristocratic town house in the centre of Vienna. The exterior design of the premises was conditioned by the style of the original building. In order to respect the structure of the house without renouncing the young and dynamic image of the company, the decision was made to create a second façade, behind the original. This second façade looks like a stage backdrop, architecturally independent of the first, and the space between the two has been converted into a large shop window display in which the mannequins are arranged and the product is exhibited.

The three floors are connected by stairs and a lift, which are completely visible from the street. The main entrance is reached across a bridge, spanning the gap between the two façades and adding an even more pronounced accentuation to the visual separation between the two.

The magnificence and theatricality of the exterior structure is in stark contrast to the simplicity of the shop window displays. Mannequins, dressed from head to foot with the company's garments, without absolutely no ornamental motifs to distract from the products on display. The lighting is based on spots suspended from the ceiling lighting fittings.

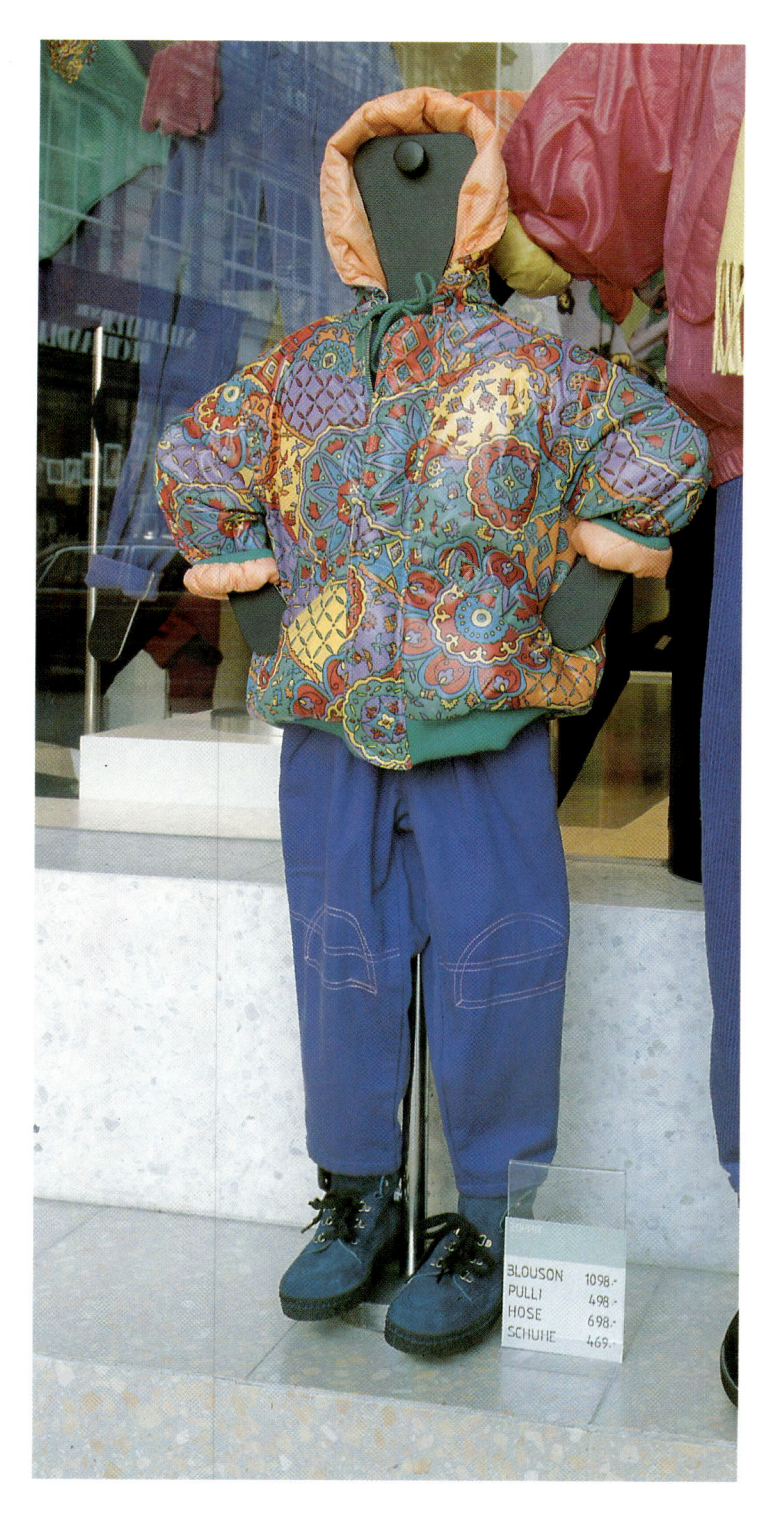

On the previous page, to the left, an exterior view of the shop during the day and lit at night, and a shot of some of the mannequins.

Also on the previous page, a floor distribution plan of the ground floor of the shop.

Some of the mannequins on display are dressed in confident and vivaciously coloured garments which impart an enormous liveliness to the composition. The black painted columns are a decorative constant throughout the shop windows and the interior display cases.

L'Observatoire

Zébu

L'Observatoire is another clear example of the shop as window display, in which practically the entire interior of the shop is visible from outside, as if it were a stage. The garments which are on display are simply draped on the floor, without any kind of ornamental support.

A view of the shop from the outside showing the simplicity and luminosity of the multi-purpose space, which has been converted into its own shop window.

Below, a view from the interior of the premises, with the garments draped on the floor behind the window. The austerity with which the clothes are displayed attracts the attention of the passers by, who are drawn remorselessly towards the clothes and then on into the interior of the shop itself.

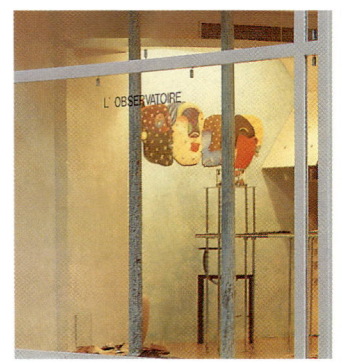

The shop window display of this boutique transcends its own limitations, occupying the whole of the commercial space, as the designers opted for the creation of an open plan, completely visible from the street through the large framed windows. Behind the glass there are only a few columns, in a blue tone which combines with the colour of the walls and converts the shop itself into a large display window.0

The premises are paved with parquet flooring and the walls and ceilings are painted with soft blue and beige tones. The halogen spots, built into the ceiling, complete a composition in which the dominant tone is that of simplicity. The garments which are on display

Various views of the establishment, both from outside and inside. On the left, the lighting system based on halogen spots is visible, while the display structures are reduced to a minimum with simple steel bars fitted to the wall and built-in shelving.

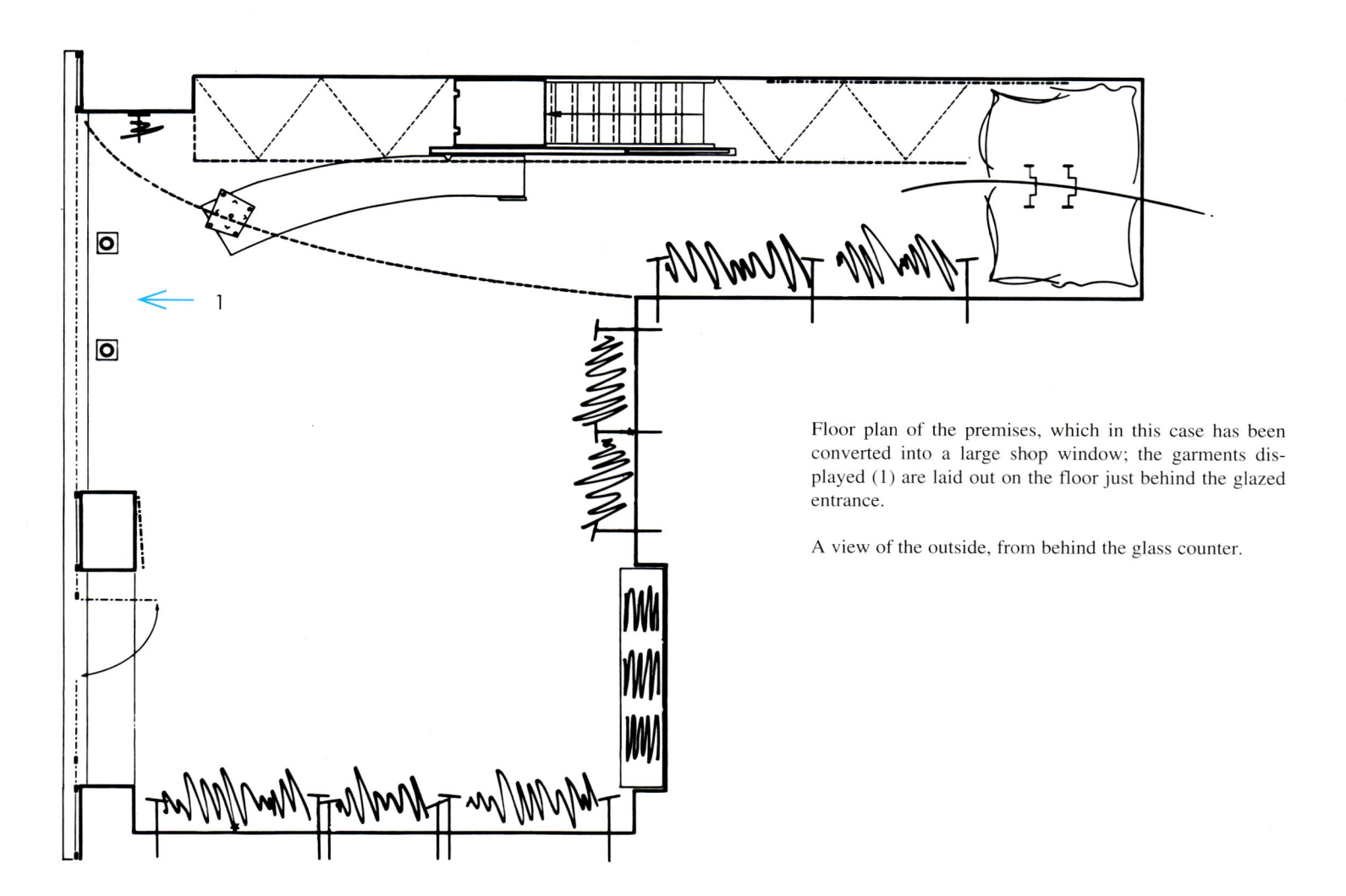

Floor plan of the premises, which in this case has been converted into a large shop window; the garments displayed (1) are laid out on the floor just behind the glazed entrance.

A view of the outside, from behind the glass counter.

are draped across the floor, without any kind of support. This creates a strong impression on passers by who, unable to see any other object, find their attention drawn to the clothes on display, or beyond into the interior of the shop itself.

The sense of harmony inspired by this simplicity of line and the attractiveness of the chromatic combination, a result of the balance between cool and warm colours, grants the window display of this shop a luminous and subtle atmosphere which touches a chord deep in the mind of the observer.

MARGARITA NUEZ

Oriol Armengou

Front view of one of the shop windows, in which the sobriety of the composition emphasises the elegance of the outfits.

On the following page, a partial view of the shop window, in which the vegetation dominates much of the decor, adding a lighter touch to the tonal severity of the garments on display.

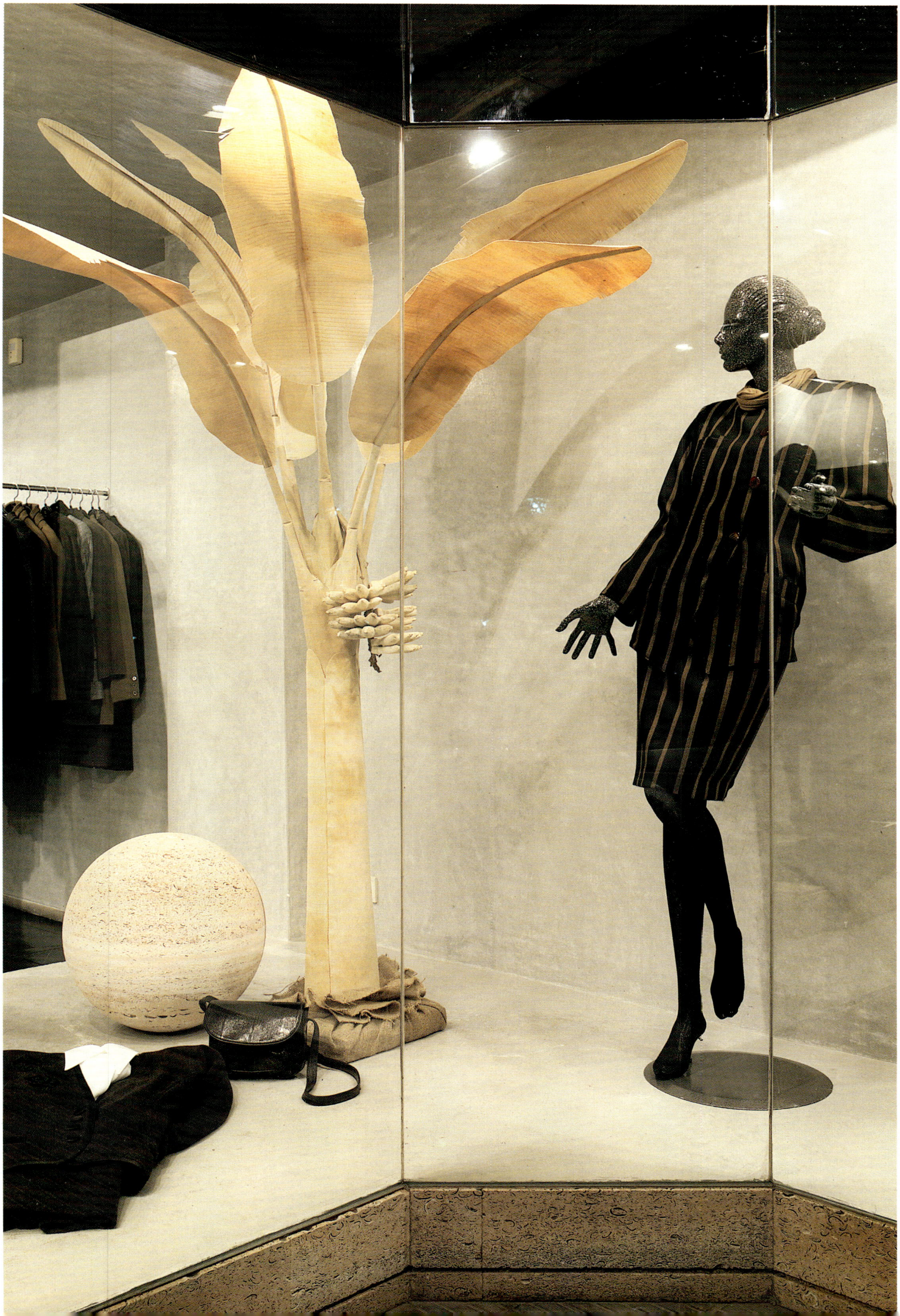

A view of the entrance and, on the right, the façade, characterised by its sobriety, discretion and elegance. On the following page, a sample of the tonal sobriety which dominates a large part of the window display.

Below, a plan of the interior, showing the window display partition with its box compartments, each of the boxes presenting a precise arrangement in both aesthetic and display terms.

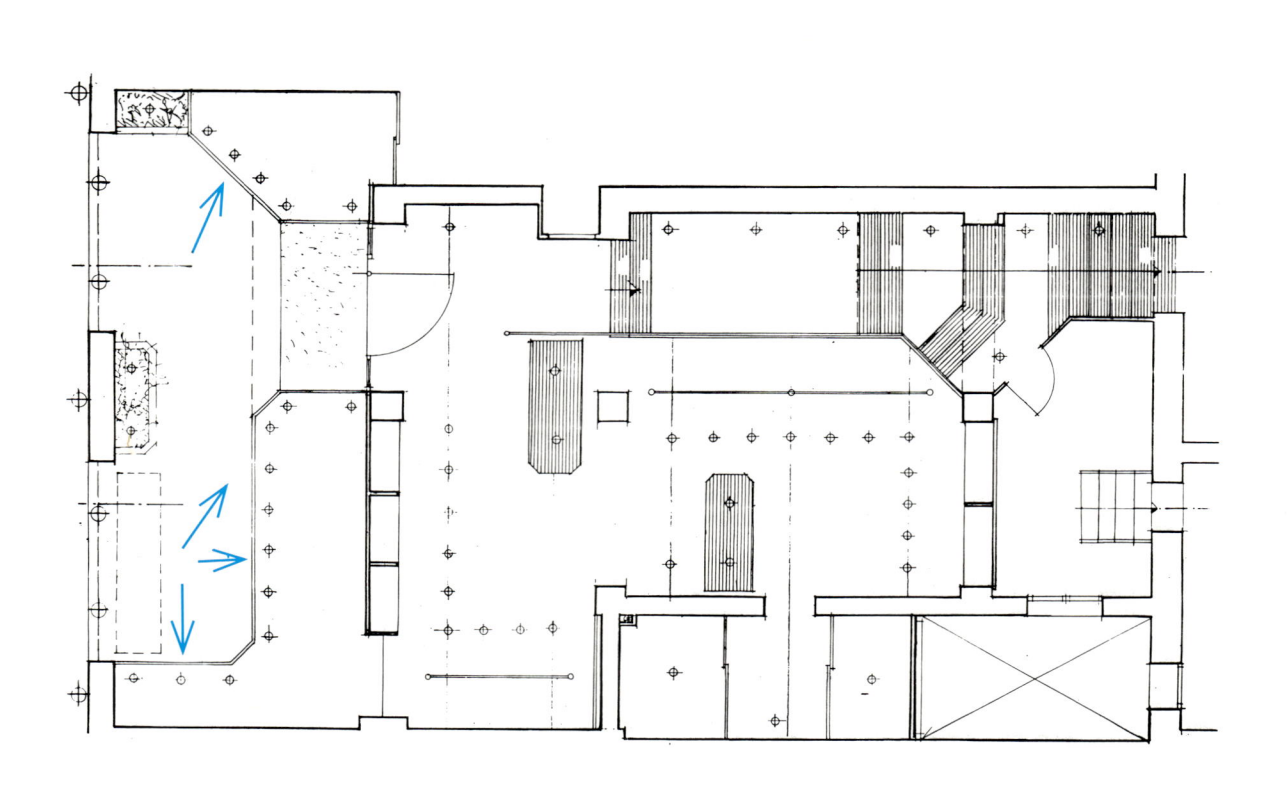

The façade of this women's fashion shop is in grey striated stone and consists of two arches, above the spans of which are glass facings bearing the sign and the trade mark of the company painted in black.

The shop windows project out in angular rectilinear outlines against a discreet light grey background, which reflects the colour of the interior ceiling and walls. The lighting is provided by an external perimeter strip of halogen lamps which bestow a high degree of clarity and transparency on the space.

The garments are arranged with a sense of separation which is further exaggerated by the size of the entrance. Other mannequins of a more lifelike appearance, in grey with silver highlights, have been added to the structural mannequins, which consist of slender wooden and metal ladders. Stands and superimposed volumes made out of blocks of pink Russian travertine, an attractive sphere and the figure of a horse are distributed in perfect harmony with the vegetation which has been arranged as a decorative element. Laid out on the floor, on the stands and even draped across the figure of the horse, the garments are allowed to shine in a proportioned isolation, granting them an importance in consonance with their evident quality.

TEHEN

Denis Colomb

A front view of the establishment, in which the symmetrical elegance of the façade is contrasted against the originality of the window display.

On the following page, one of the mannequins dressed in an *haute couture* model and accompanied by a plant, these being the only ornamental elements on view. The practical nonexistence of scenographic complements is a constant in the decoration of Tehen shop window displays.

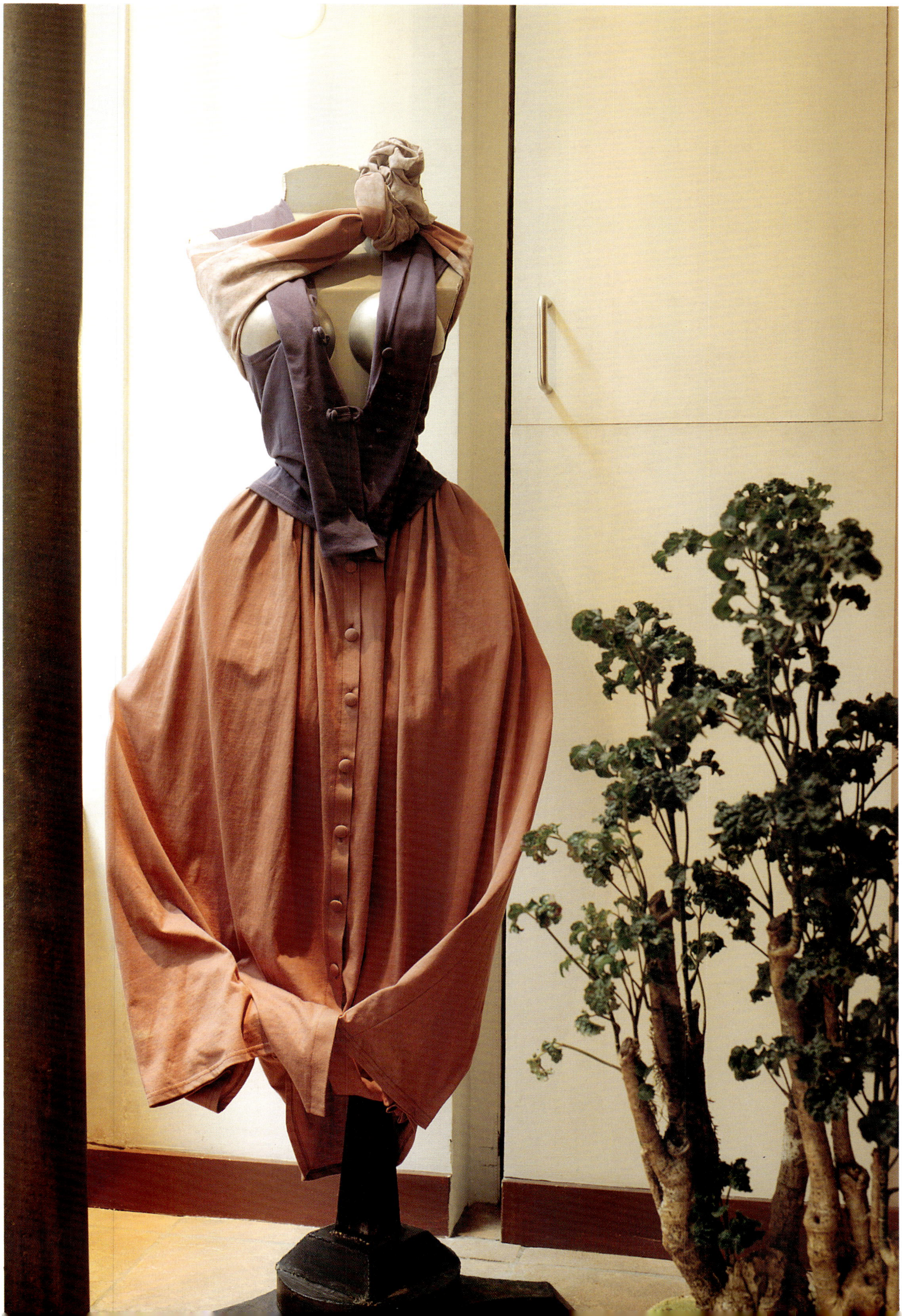

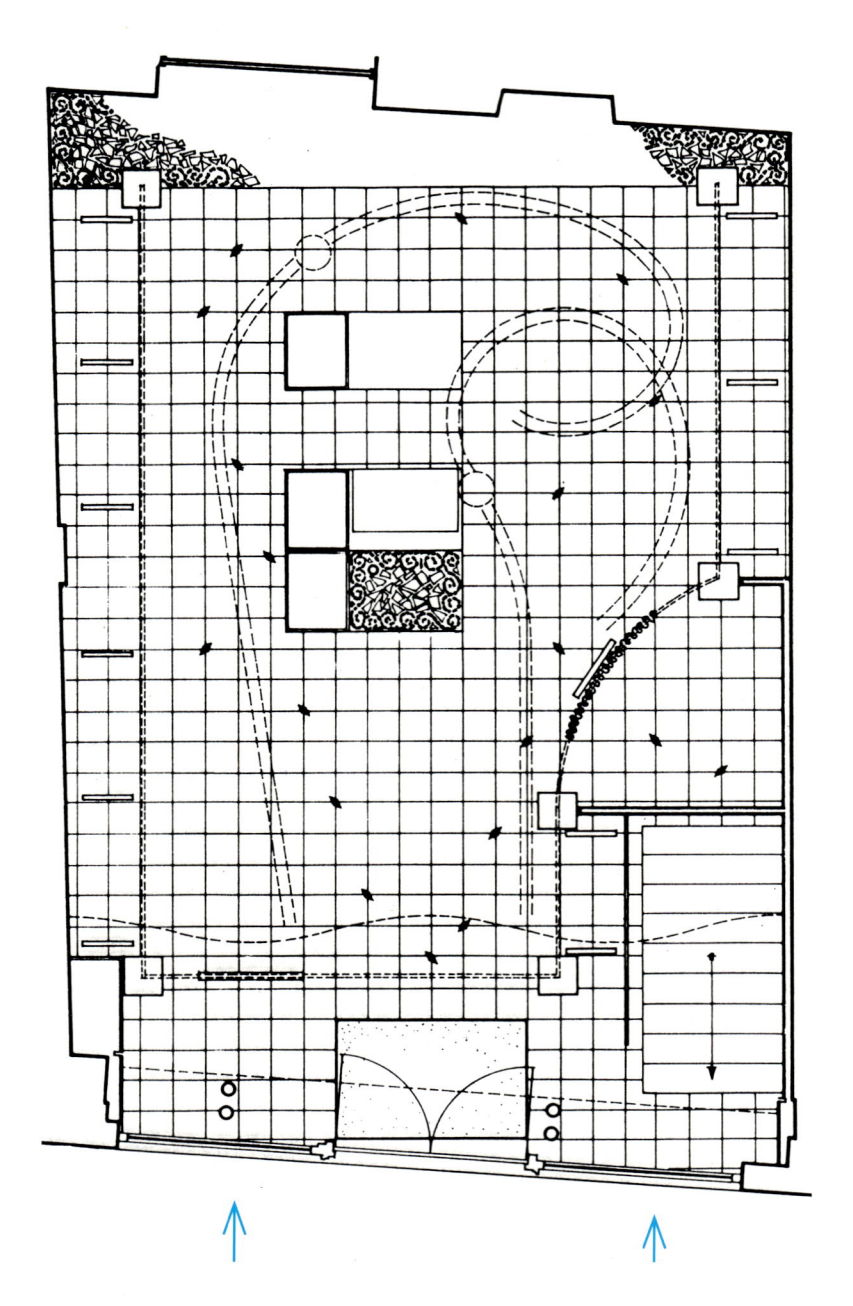

A distribution plan of the shop, with the window display indicated with arrows.

Tehen is a notably atypical shop, mixing a large dose of design with a functionalism which is relative and relegated to a second plane. Two windows frame a seemingly welcoming entrance, which turns out to have an icy and distant feel as a result of the materials used: Venetian glass, ceramic and metal.

In terms of the tendency in window dressing which it represents, there is a simple elegance reflecting the image of this designer company which is outstanding. In the eyes of the observer a lone model appears, breathing *haute couture* from every pore, and on the other side, there is a preliminary sketch of another of the designs. These two singular elements, lacking any kind of decoration or additional objects as an aesthetic support, are located in two of the corners of the windows, projecting the interior of the shop out towards the exterior, with all the appearance of an explosion of aesthetic composition.

The shop as window display, or internal window dressin, prevails here, and in this context mention must be made of the contrived simplicity of the arrangement and the importance of the decor, which is directly related to the architectural project itself, devoid of complications or scenographic details. The mannequins are made of metal in

On the following page, above, tiled shelves which function both as a display surface and an ornamental element. Below, a garment draped on one of the ledges, its black colour clearly contrasted against the light tone of the ceramic tiles.

90

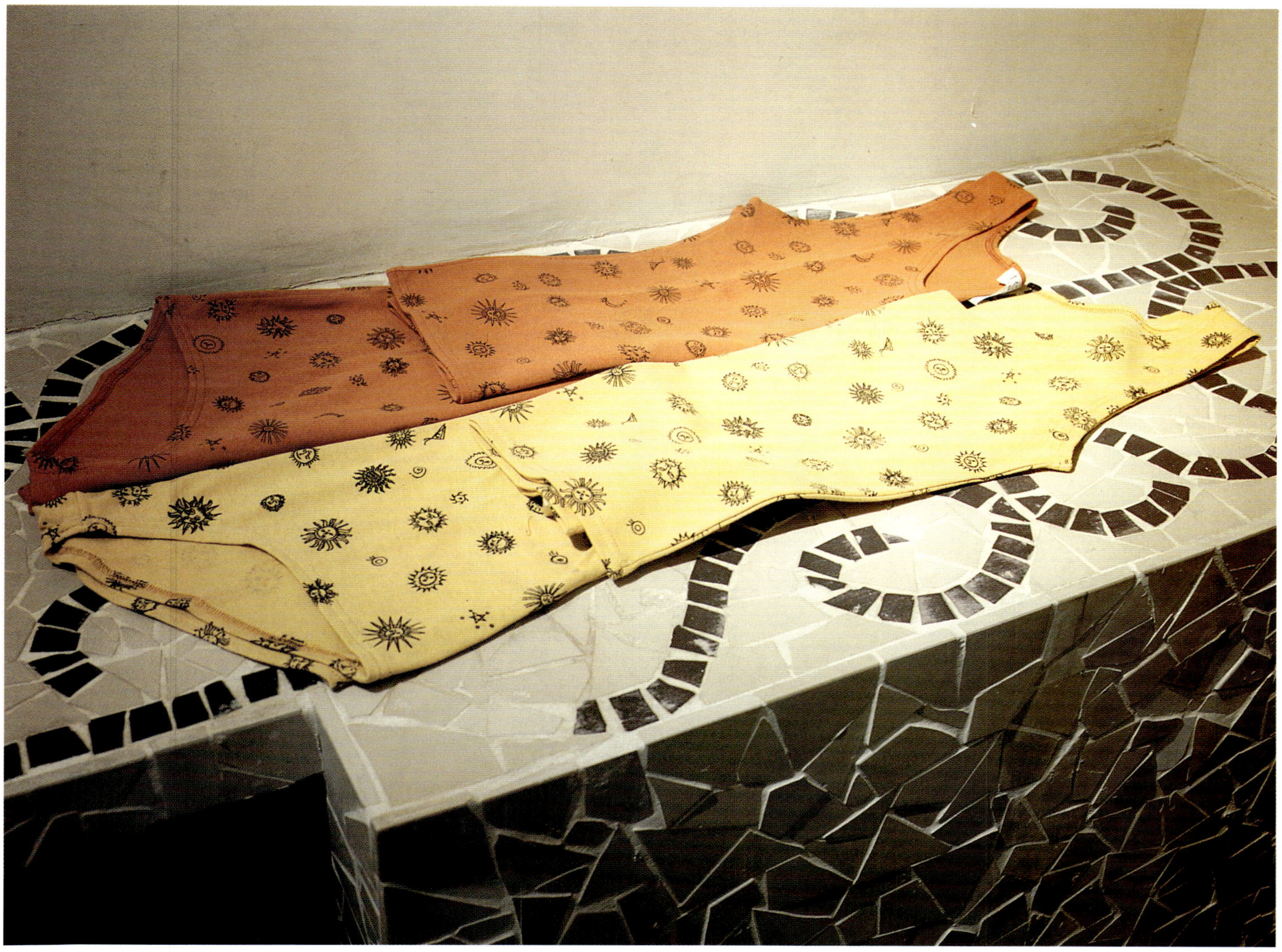

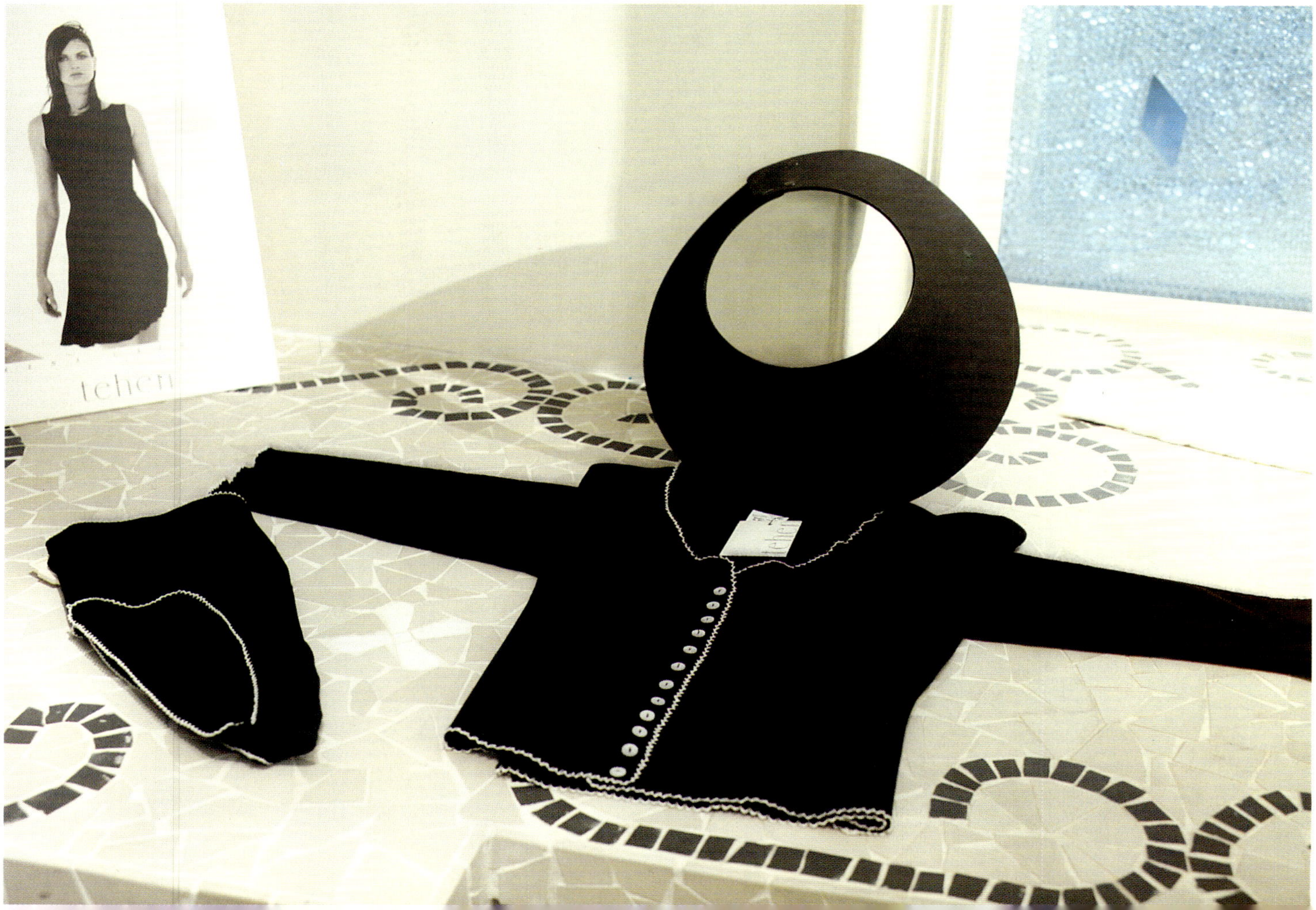
tehen

a variety of tones, and for the clothes which are laid out horizontally, use is made of the ledges, with their tile mosaic in circular designs. Glass display cases, which function as more conventional window displays, back onto the sales counter where garments and complementary accessories are displayed.

Finally, a brief description of the symmetrical arrangement of the clothes: the articles which are not worn by the mannequins adopt their own postures on the window ledges and shelves. The clothes-racks, installed in the walls, also play an important role in the overall display as a result of their arrangement and contents.

On this page, some of the display counters in the interior of the shop are illustrated: glass showcases (below) and supports which evoke the female body (above). The latter have a display character which is more aesthetic than functional, often acting more as sculptures than supports.

On the following page, a view of the shop window from the interior, illustrating the columns which were erected to maintain the visual balance between the historic façade and the innovative and cool design of the shop itself.

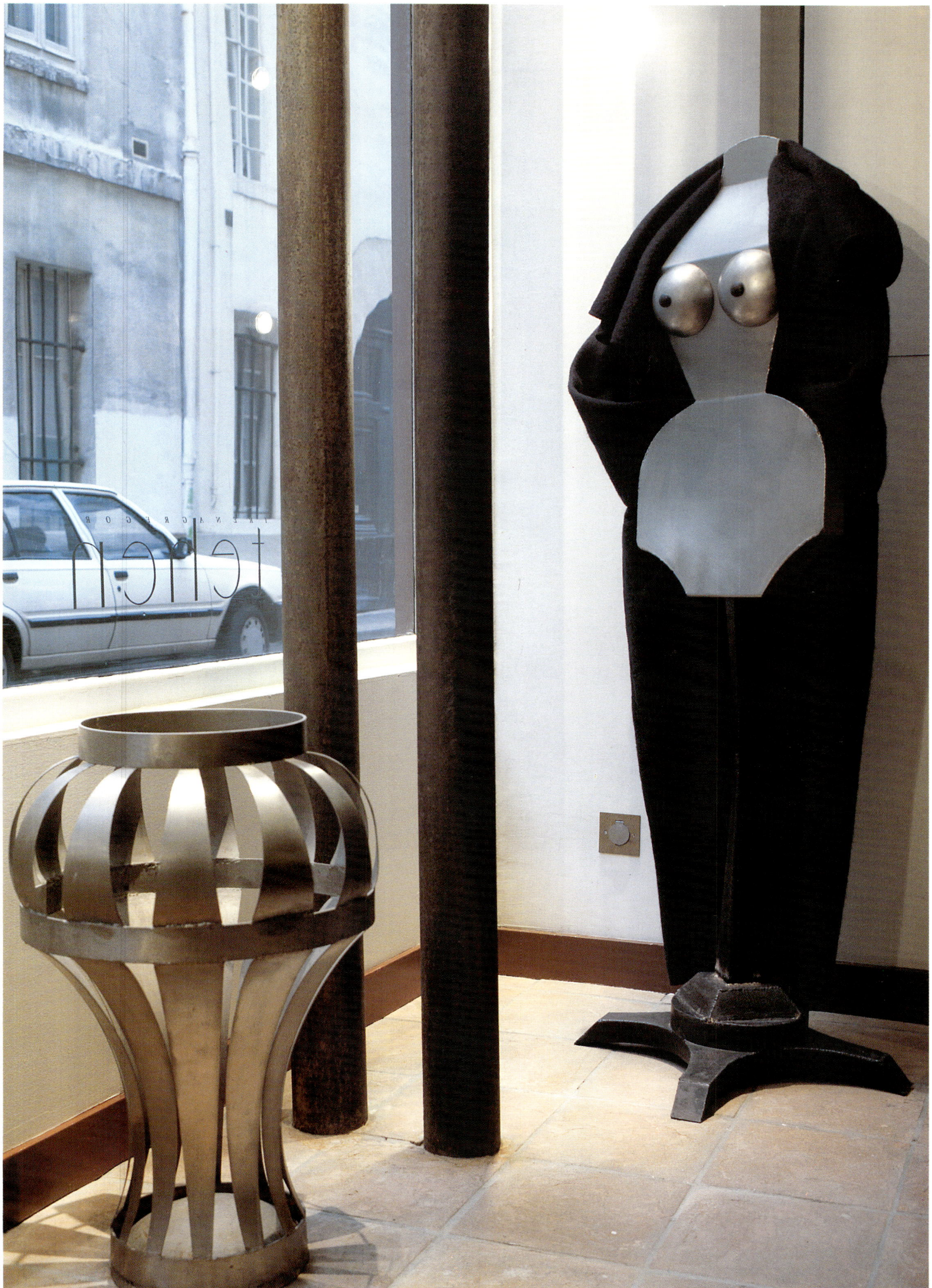

ALEXANDER

Wolfgang Graswander

A view of one of the shop window display areas, with a horizontal style of exhibition and irregular characteristics, both in terms of the window itself and the display in the area behind.

Next page: a view of the shop window from the interior of the shop with the articles draped across the main dais, and with the counter running the length of the area on the left, which serves as a backup for both interior and exterior display.

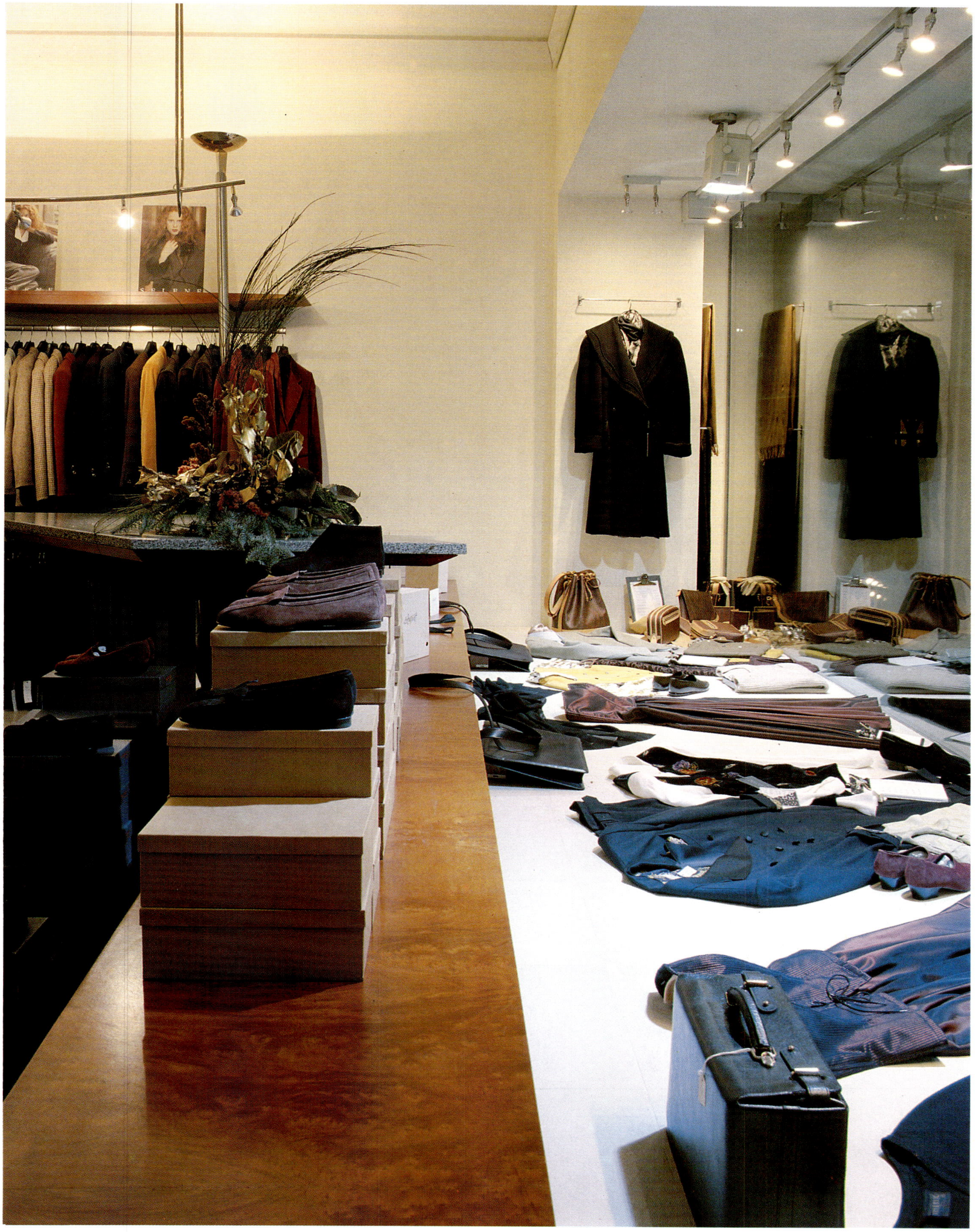

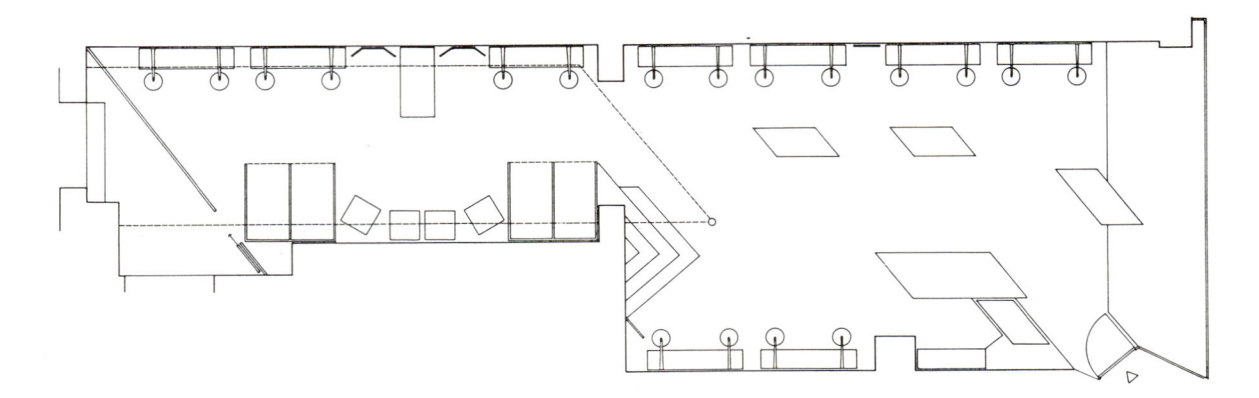

A distribution plan of Alexander.

Facing the street, the display forms a huge showcase which contains the display area, at mid height, enabling it to be looked down on from above.

The entrance door forms a strangely acute angle, penetrating into the interior of the shop itself. This is the only entrance and is located at the far end of the elongated display window.

The modernity of the style of the Alexander shop contrasts with the cliched view of a central European women's fashion shop. The entrance doorway is located at the end of a lengthy façade which forms an acute angle cutting in towards the interior of the shop. The shop's trademark is screen printed onto the entrance, also appearing on one of the side areas, in the form of metallic letters.

The totality of the façade of the Alexander shop consists of an enormous window which gives out onto the street, and is scarcely divided visually by a metal band which forms a part of the frame. The window display was defined, at mid height, in a way that not only added to an expositive vision, but symbolically opens the doors of the premises to the passers by. It is not just a matter of a visual access which stimulates the curiosity, but of the lack of conventionality of the interior design which invites the perception and contemplation of the interior display areas.

In terms of style, behind the area of the windows a base is extended horizontally, running along the length of the window, and directly on top of which different garments

A partial view of an area of the shop window, in which the display criterion is that of surrounding a central article with others which are complementary to it, yet without reinforcing the first at the expense of the others; commercial importance is granted equally to all the articles.

On the following page, two shots of the same display area; above, a view from the interior and, below, from the street.

are draped without supports or aesthetic backups of any kind. There are only a few articles on display, but the rigid and uneven arrangement differentiates them as individual units of an essential quality. The spatial isolation of the garments hung from the side walls of the window display is not coincidental, but an intentional expression of the desire to highlight and emphasise the design and quality of these pieces.

Immediately behind the window an elongated counter, facing the interior, displays a series of articles and boxes stored in full view. The distribution of the elements usually consists of important garments, but without the expression of any individual preference, reinforcing the excellence of each piece.

The main shop window display and the elongated counter complete the display space, which extends further into the interior with a variety of different units, combining shelves and racks. To the generally cool atmosphere of the premises, with their steel and wooden components contrasted against the grey and beige of the walls, a warmer lighting based on halogen lamps, which reflect up towards the ceiling, and strips of directional spots, introduces a stark counterpoint.

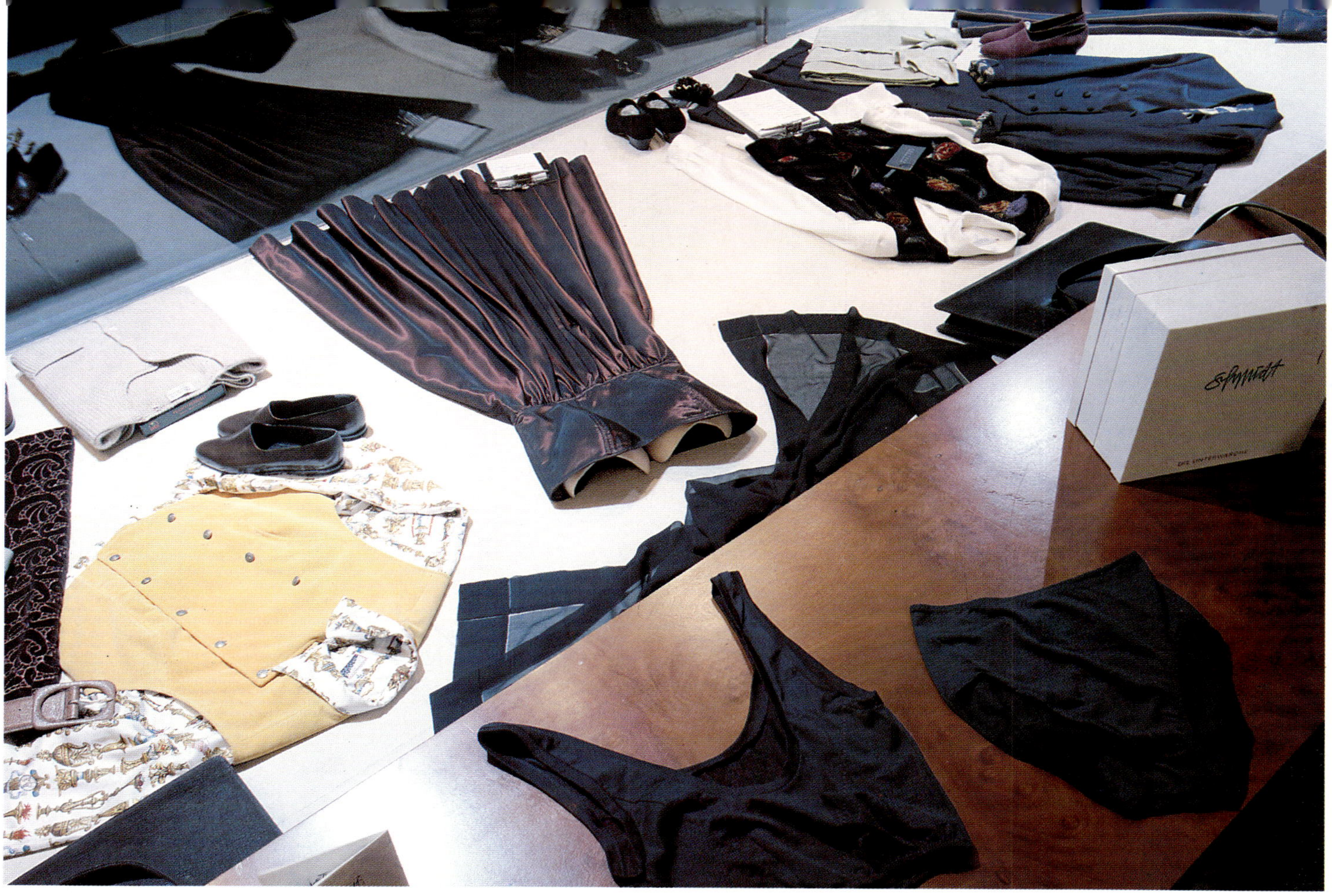

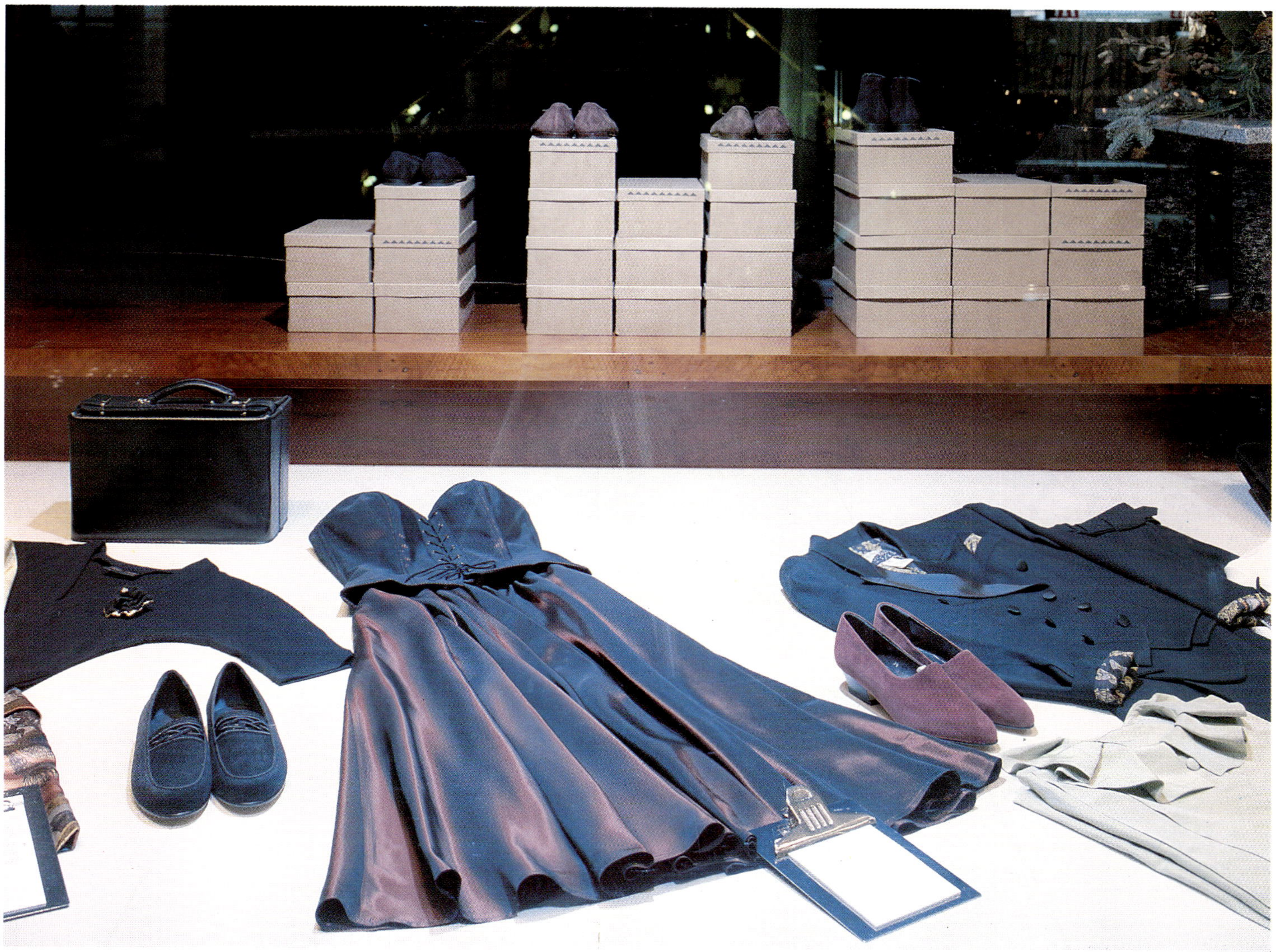

JEAN-CHARLES DE CASTELBAJAC

Patrick de Maupeou

The left-hand part of the display window, seen from the interior of the shop. It is characterised by a richly varied, self-assured and showy decor, with a stunning printed carpet and a brightly coloured umbrella, together with a profusion of puppets representing Snoopy, a well-known canine character.

On the following page, one of the light-coloured wooden mannequins with a circular base which constitute the main supports for the garments on display.

This innovative and imaginative French designer's shop is not limited to the display and sale of fashion; it also sells carpets, sofas, settees, tableware, furniture generally and a great variety of original design work.

The cement façade presents two openings in which a shop window and the access door have been installed, on the left, and a second shop window on the right. A white sign is mounted on a mirrored wall facing above the door, and an inscription on one of the transversal blocks of the separating partition wall identifies the premises.

The constant allusion in the work of Castelbajac to the primary colours in their brightest tones is illustrated here by the intermingling coloured spots located in the window displays. Inside the premises, these are the protagonists of the discreet interruptions which have been introduced by the insertion of dayglo tiles in green, red, yellow and blue in the islands of parquet surrounded by the main flooring element of painted cement.

The display space of the shop windows is divided by vertical white-painted pipes in the form of small columns. The decor of the two shop windows is extremely original, while the bags display, located at the back of the premises, is more closely aligned with the classical concept of a display.

The lighting is based on directional and built-in halogen spots which create a recreational and attractive atmosphere.

On the right, part of the left-hand window display, with the multi-coloured carpet on the floor and the garments worn by the mannequin and draped across the two brightly coloured settees. A painted wooden silhouette in the form of a caricature (not visible in the photo) completes the composition. The lighting is provided by spots suspended from the ceiling, although only a low lighting intensity is needed during the day due to the abundance of natural light entering through the windows.

Below, two of the mannequins dressed in original, even surprising, garments, such as the red coat on the right, and accompanied by painted wooden figures, such as the stag and the child.

On the following page, the window display on the right of the entrance, the sobriety of which contrasts with the decorative explosion of the window display to the right. The wooden shelf with the display of bags, all in soft brown and beige tones, with an occasional detail in black, add a note of seriousness to the space.

102

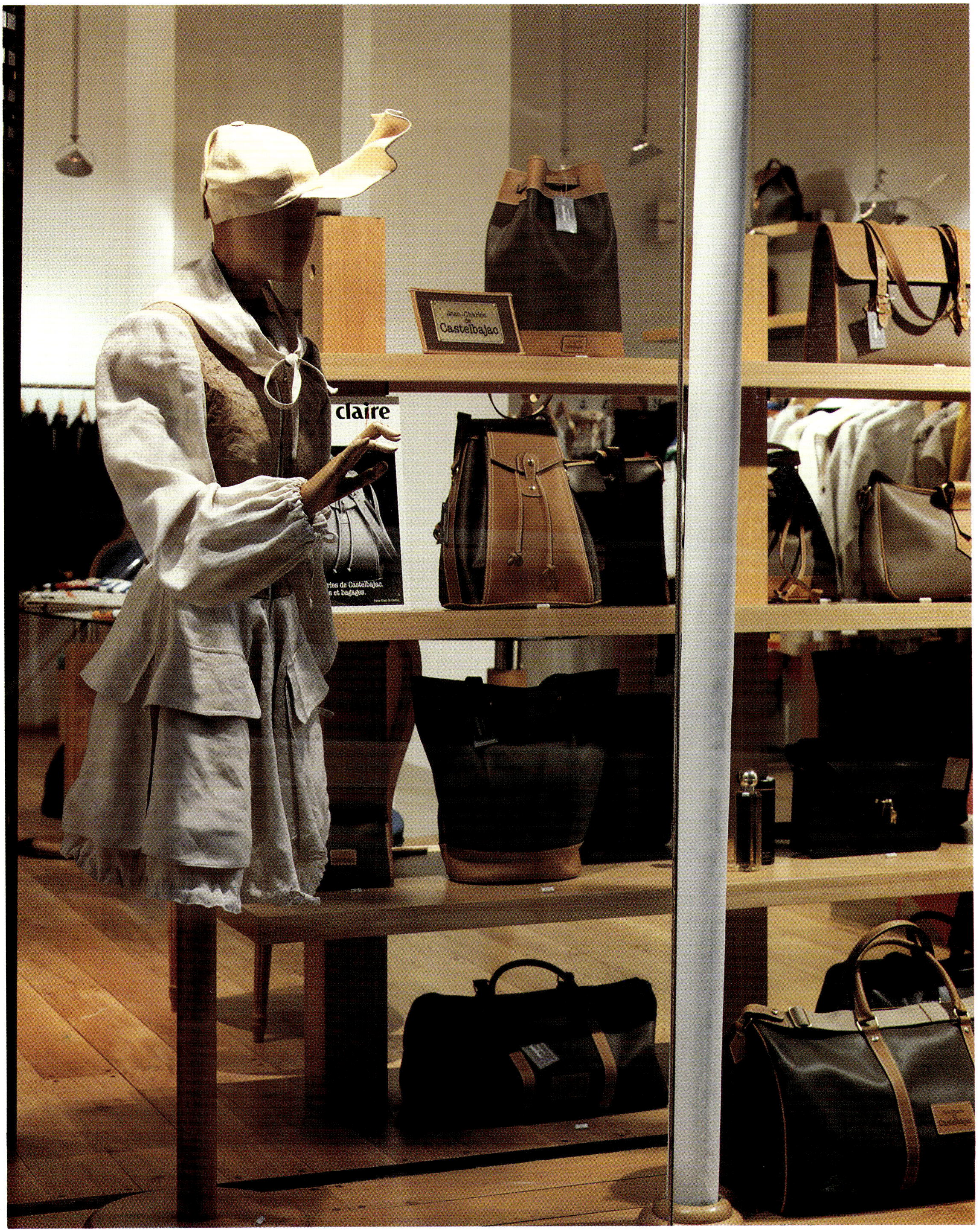
Jean-Charles
de
Castelbajac
claire

GIANFRANCO FERRÉ

Letizia Caruzzo, Paolo C. Rancati & Ezio Riva, Architetti Associati

A view of one of the main window displays, illustrating the original disposition of the garments around the conceptual mannequin, highlighted by the halogen light which is emitted by spots located in recesses in the walls.

Next page: the strange composition of the window display, with the shoes occupying the space where the head of the mannequin should be, is aimed at attracting attention of passers by.

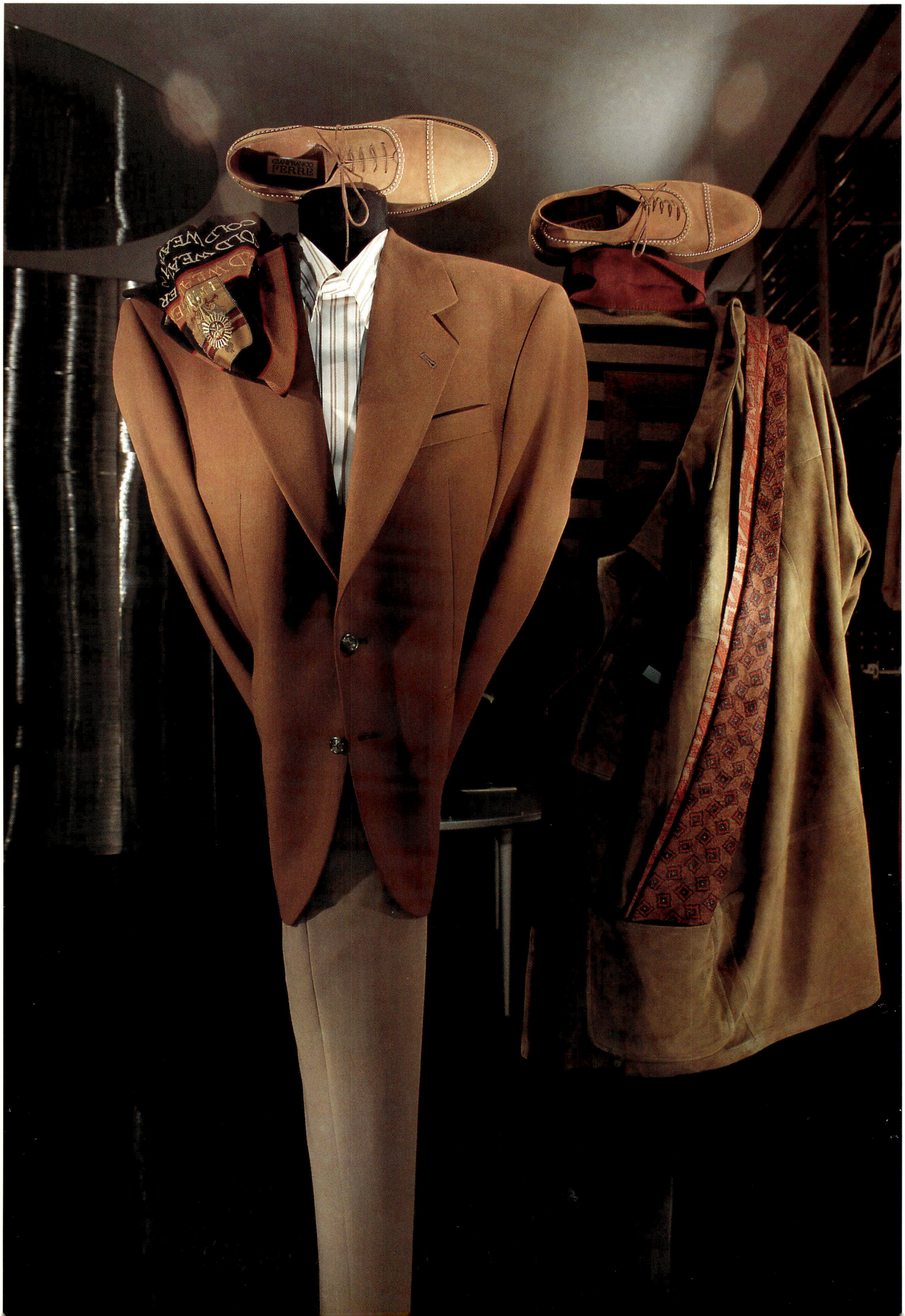

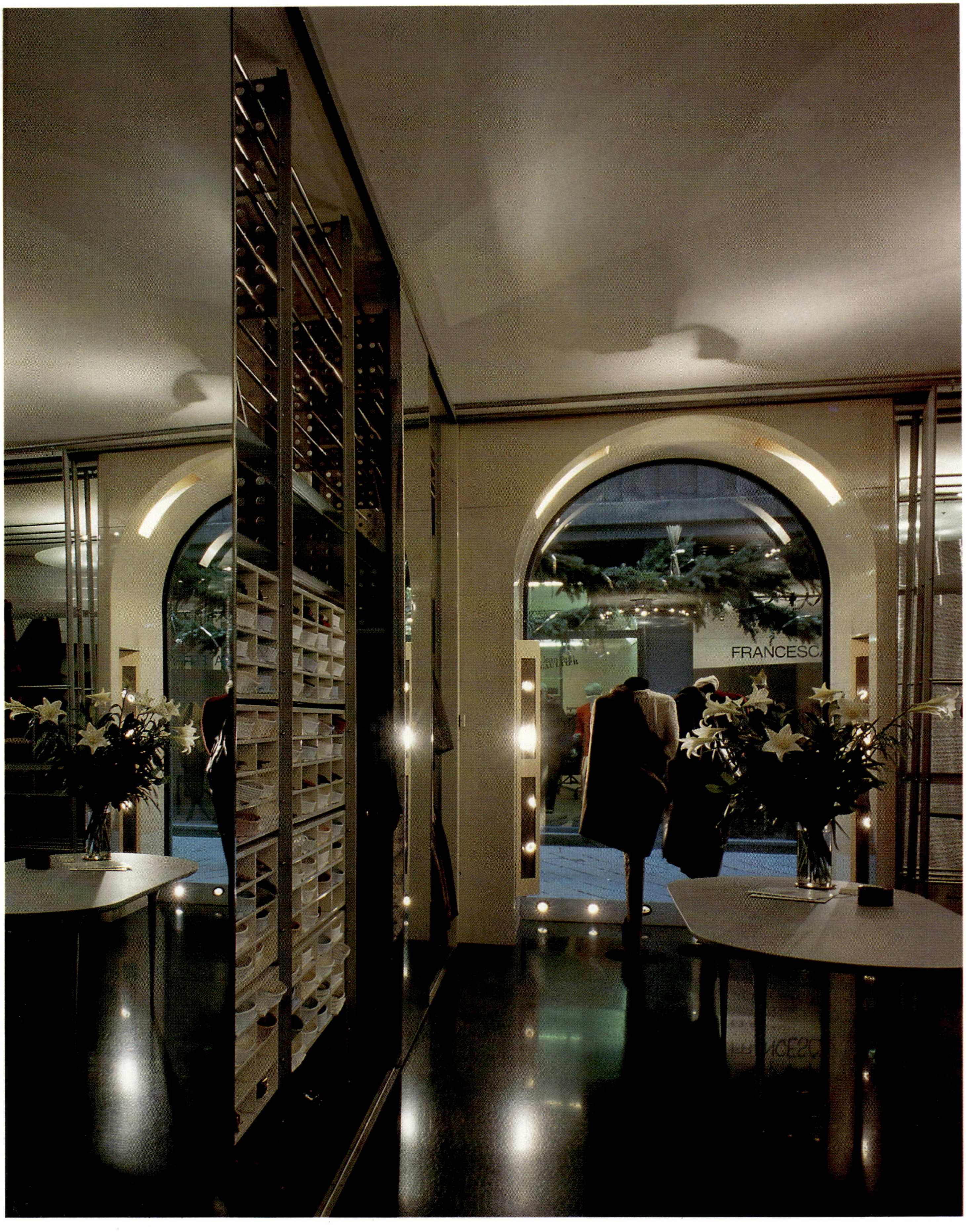

On the previous page, a view of the window display from inside the establishment illustrating its direct accessibility, without any physical separation, and the lighting which is aimed at emphasising the importance of the articles on display.

On this page, a detail of one of the mannequins and, on the right, a view of the façade during the day and at night, lit by three directional spots over the two arches and the entrance, and by the light from the shop windows.

On the following page, the arrangement of the garments on the mannequins, based on absolutely innovative and original guidelines which infringe the laws of logic, but which succeed in capturing the attention of the passer by.

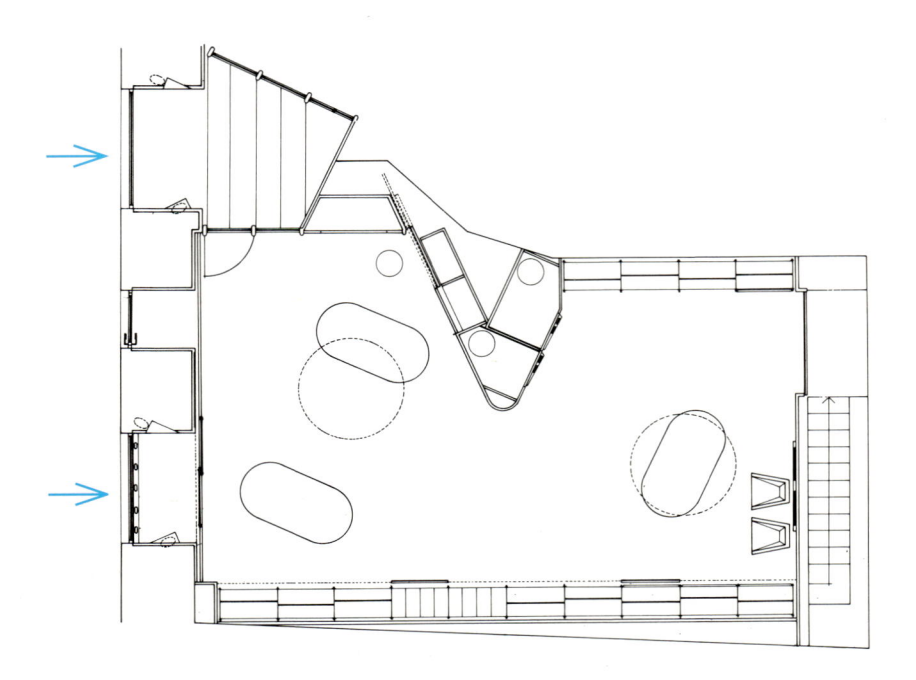

A floor plan of the shop with the window display areas indicated with arrows.

In the course of his investigation into forms and materials Gianfranco Ferré has always expressed his ambition to achieve a symbiosis of tradition and experimentalism, and this is reflected in the architectural, spatial and aesthetic forms which proliferate in his shop in Milan.

The main entrance is in the façade, flanked by two large arched windows, fully glazed, which form the perfect frame for the main shop window displays.

The window display space features only an arrangement of busts which are mounted on original pillars of black metal. The clothes are arranged on these busts in a manner which intentionally infringes the laws of logic and with the aim of attracting the attention of the passer by. Thus the articles are superimposed on the mannequins, tied to the back, the shoes are placed where the head should be, a bunch of ties run diagonally across the front of a jacket like a sash, and one mannequin is placed face on while another has its back turned.

Halogen lamps hidden within recesses in the wall, some at the side and others almost at floor level, light the shop window, emphasising the importance of the garments which are being displayed, with no other motif to distract from their visual contemplation. The name of the designer, screen printed onto the windows, completes the sparse decoration of the area.

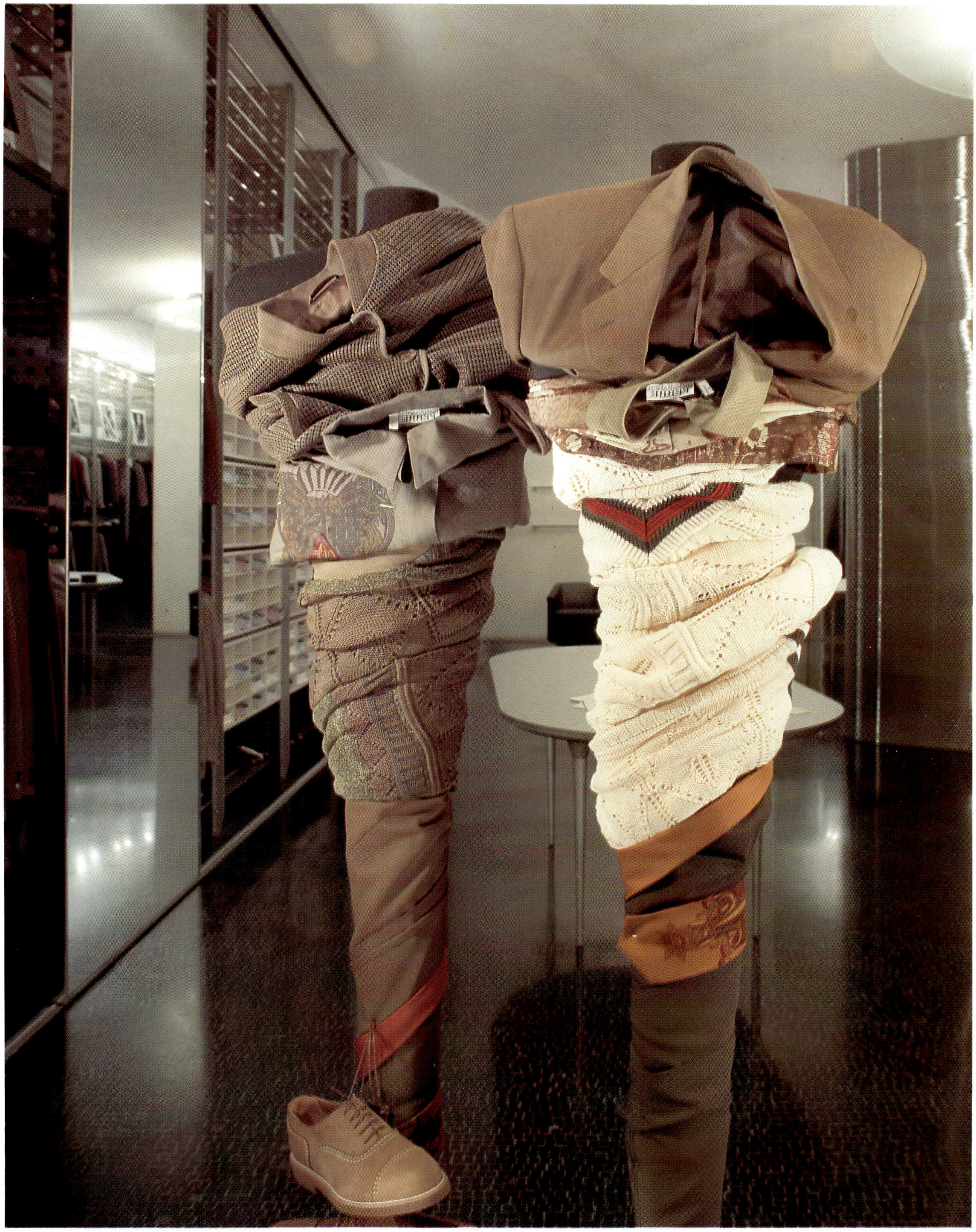

LONDON HOUSE

Federico Correa

A view of the shop window display, the transparency of which allows for a clear view of the interior of the shop, which is converted into a window display for itself.

On the following page, a shot of some of the mannequins, at the feet of which a profusion of complementary accessories for men are spread, including everything from a watch to a liquor flask.

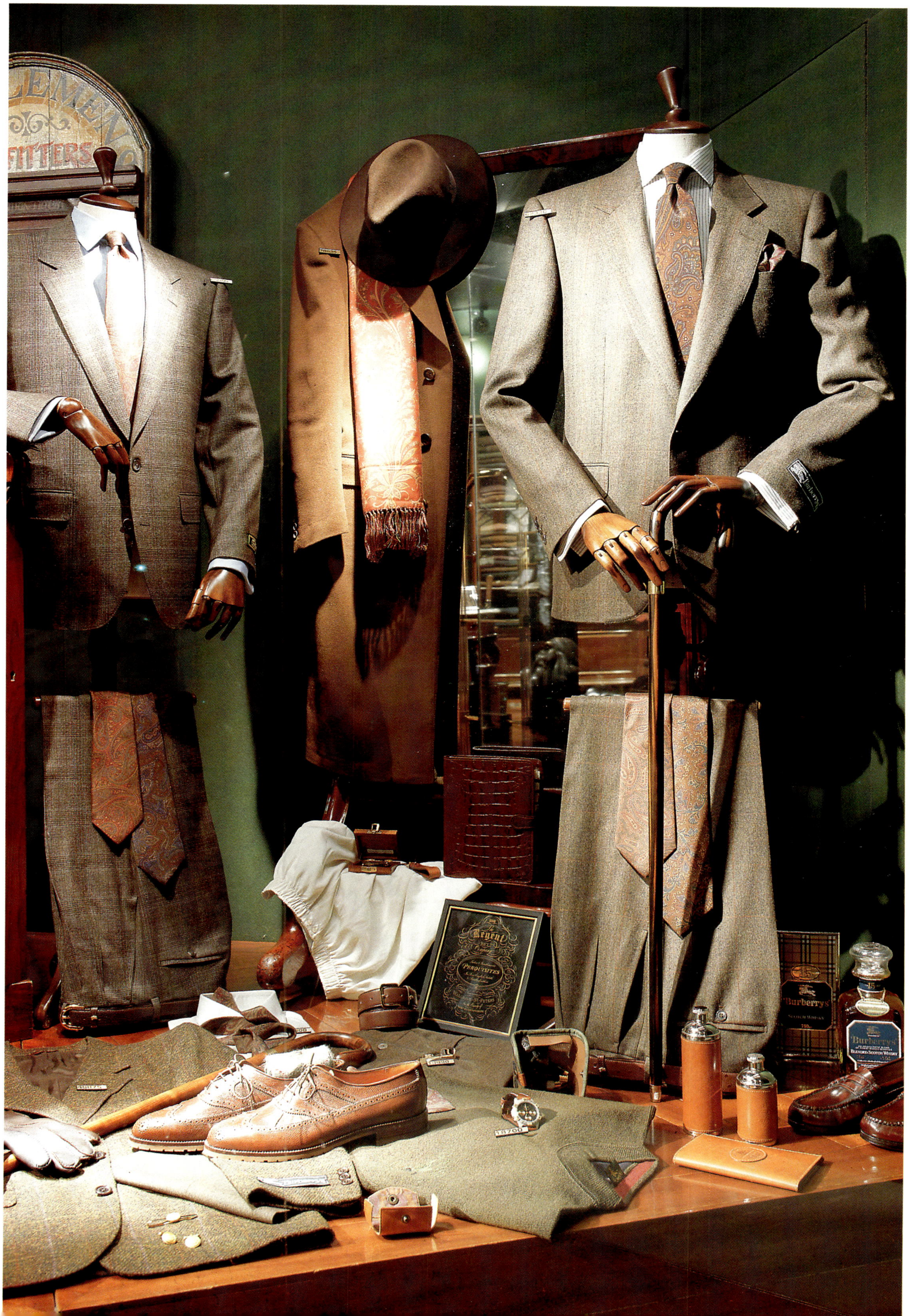
FITTERS
Burberrys

The interior re-creates a warm, classically British style.

On the sofa, which serves as a display support in the shop window, a wide variety of men's fashion garments are displayed. The direct lighting emphasises the textures of the fabrics.

The halogen spots suspended from the ceiling create an atmosphere which is intimate and welcoming. In the small photo, a view of the facade of the shop with the awning in the foreground.

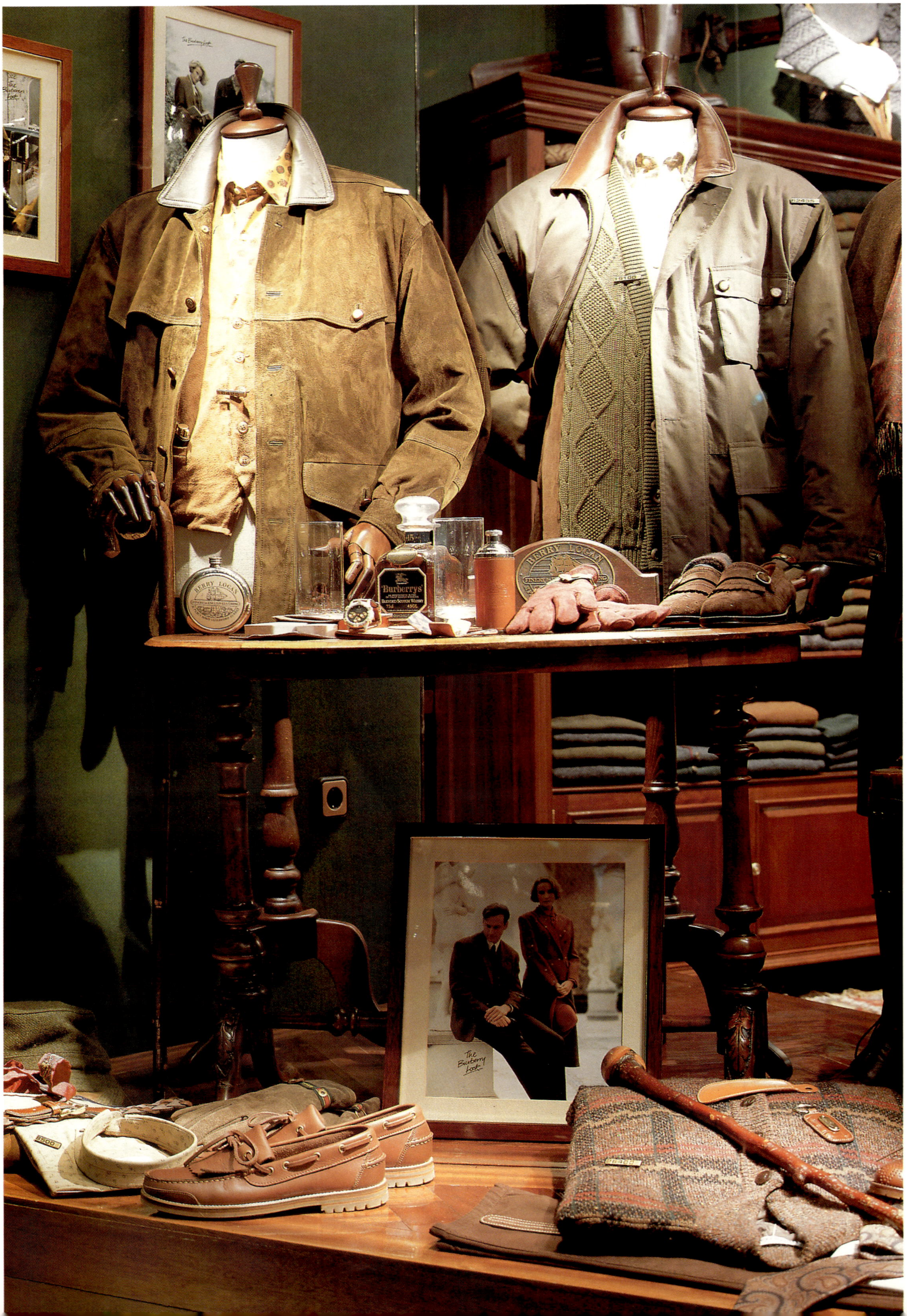

The variety of garments and complementary accessories is a constant in the decor of both the window displays and the interior of the shop. Books, wallets, walking sticks, whisky bottles and pictures become decorative elements of great expressive force.

This men's fashion shop has an English name although it does not belong to any franchise; it is a Spanish boutique which is based on a classical British model in terms of decor and style.

The façade is of transparent glass with a small green awning extended from the wall of the building, on which the name of the company is printed together with the trademark designed by the owner. A structure has been chosen which allows for space to be gained at the entrance, this being in the form of a central passageway with a door at the end, flanked by two window display areas. The transparency of the window displays allows a view of the whole of the establishment, converting it into a complete display area.

The decor is based on antique-style furnishings in a modern environment. There is a certain theatrical interplay between the two concepts, a typically English irony. The general tendency is to convert the whole of the premises into a display area and the furnishings are almost exclusively destined to that end.

In the main window display there is a traditional wooden table and a sumptuous sofa which serves as a base for the display of a wide range of garments and complementary accessories. The walls are clad with green cloth, which gives contrast to the tones of the garments, which generally fall within a range of browns and ochres. The lighting is based on directional spots of different sizes, and halogen lamps built into the ceiling.

FUJIWARA

Shimizu, Hisada & Sato

The Fujiwara shop window has no backdrop, allowing the interior arrangement, in which straight lines and an austere and elegant decor predominate, to be seen. The lighting contributes to the creation of an intimate atmosphere, thanks to an ambient white light which shines down from the ceiling spots, while these are complemented by other spots directed towards specific points.

Different shots of the interior and exterior of the shop.

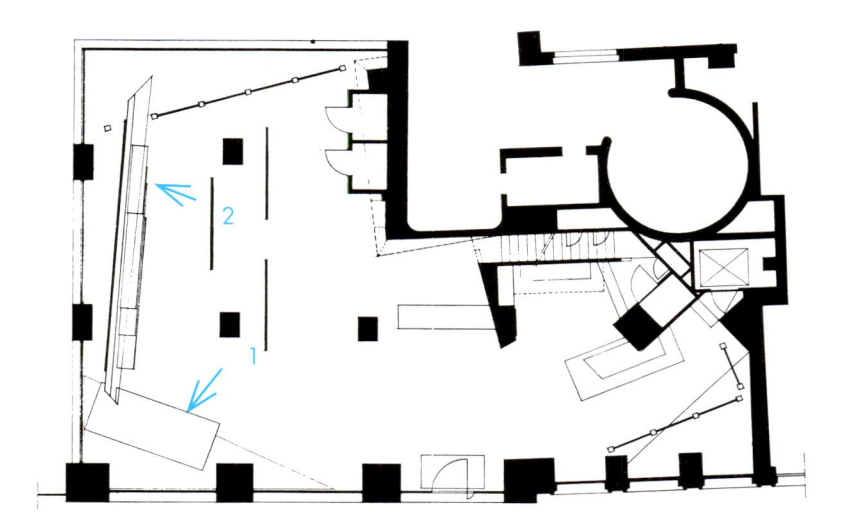

Floor plan, to the left of which is the main shop window. This is an example which reflects many of the determining elements of the composition and development of a good window display: simplicity, unity of conception, relation between form and background, a precise treatment of light and colour, and a style which is at one with the spirit of the firm. A technical aspect of great importance is evident here, the accessibility of the shop window from the interior, allowed for by the absence of a separating partition in (1) and by a side entry in (2).

A view of the window display from the outside, with the trademark featured on the window.

On this page and the page following, views of the shop's window displays from the interior, illustrating the ease of access. The various elements are arranged in a balanced and asymmetric composition which is sustained on opaque glass platforms. Elegance is the predominant note in the overall presentation.

The creations of Giuliano Fujiwara are born out of a fusion of Italian classicism and a modern sensibility, and it was this spirit which influenced the design of the space where his clothes are sold. Classicism is the source of the fine quality materials which are used, such as the mosaic and marble, and modernity is found in the abstract geometric forms of the furnishings.

The shop window display is completely glazed with no depth, allowing a view of the poised, elegant and balanced interior, with a predominance of straight lines. Three types of combined display elements are located here: opaque glass platforms, located a little above floor level; steel bars arranged in parallel, and running crosswise; and iron frames.

In one part of the window display an original terrazzo-lined wall, finished with inclined edges that perform a double function, has been added. From the outside it serves as the backdrop to the display bars, and from the interior it acts as a support for shelves made of iron plate. The garments are presented in a way that exaggerates the spacing, and as a result each article is given its own particular protagonism and the observer is required to linger in his contemplation.

Lighting is the vehicle which allows for the emphasis of the basic volumes of the space and the delineation and the highlighting of the clothes at an intensity which favours the projection of shadows and contrasts, emphasising the importance of the articles.

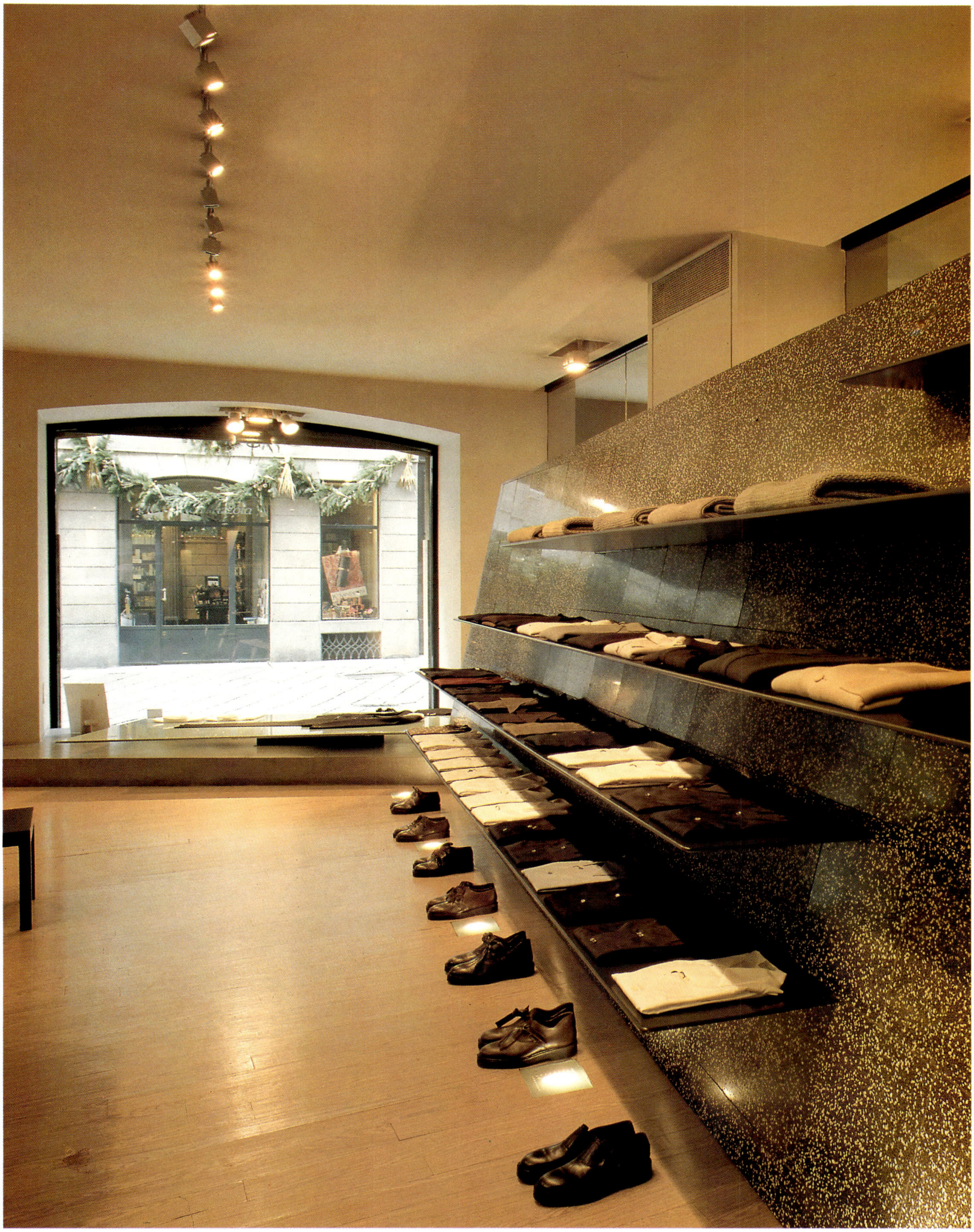

Henry Cotton's

Olivier Billiotte

To gain access to the interior of the shop it is necessary to pass through a double entrance, first a passage flanked by shop windows, and then a small patio where the true access to the shop is found.

On the following page, an area of the interior which is fitted out in the form of a display, recreating a scene as a frame for the clothes. The use of an absolutely realistic decoration is a recurrent motif both in the window displays and in the various parts of the shop which are fitted out for this purpose.

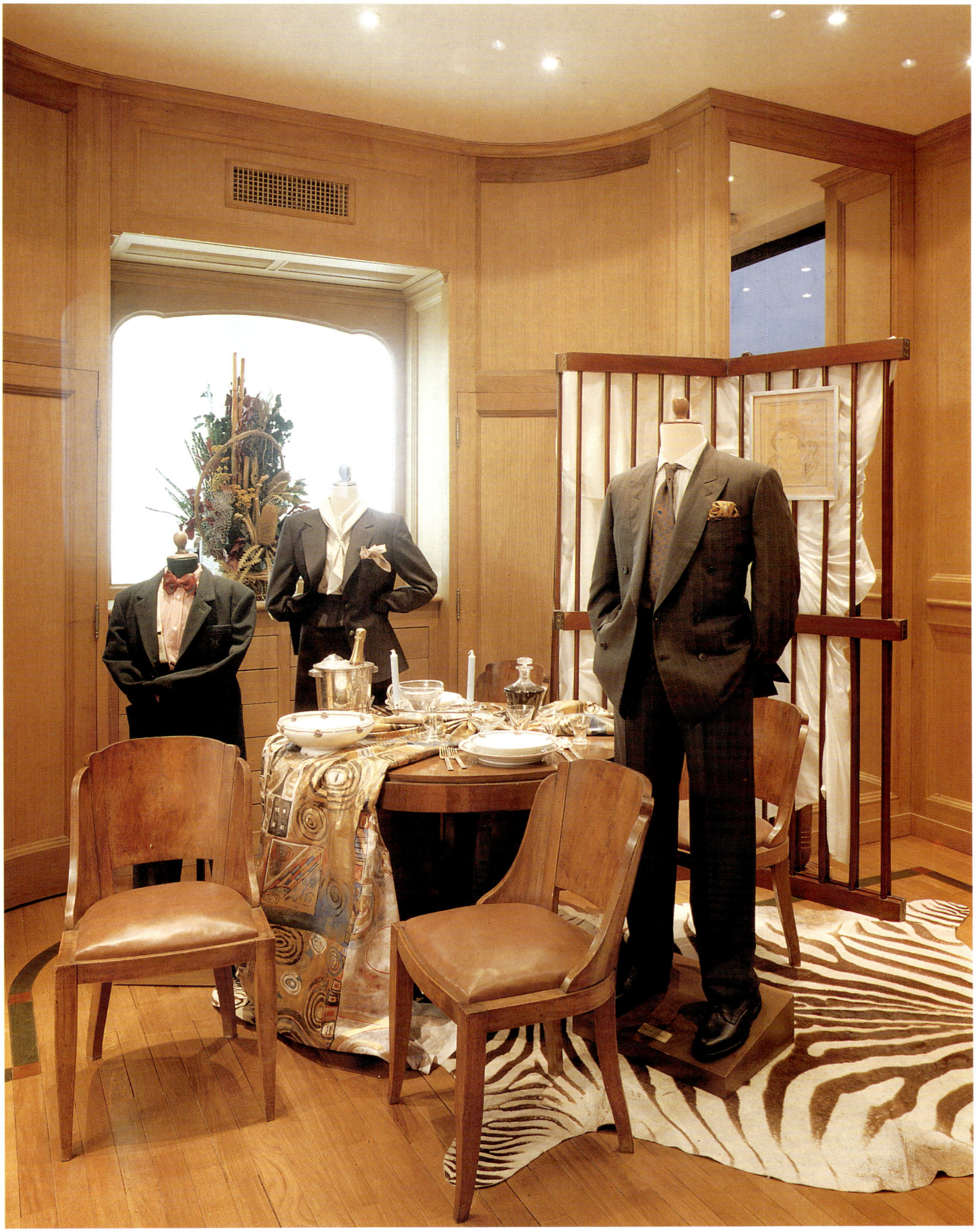

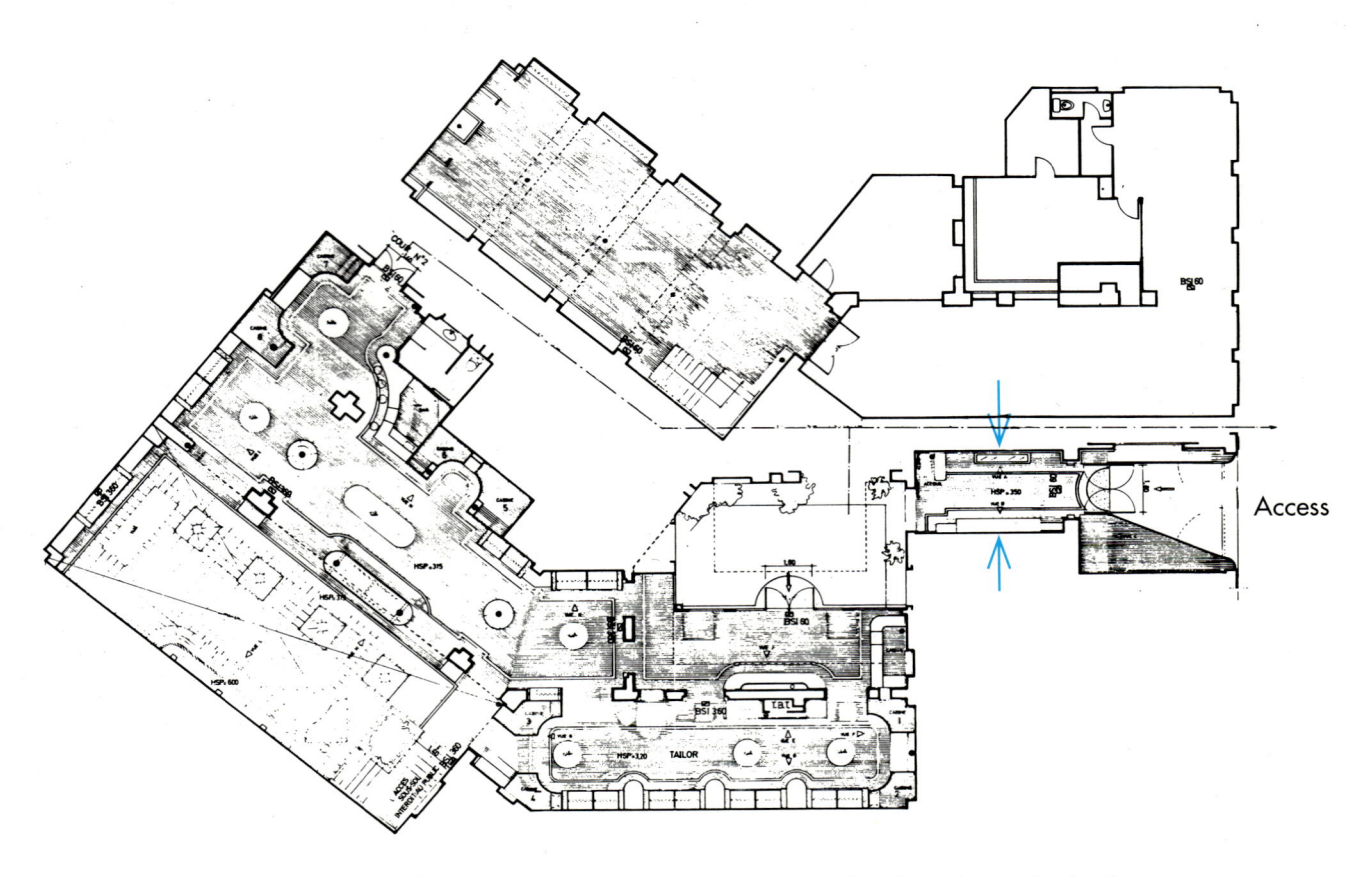

In order to gain access to the interior of this shop a double entrance must be crossed. From the street a vestibule is entered which features window displays on both sides. At the end there is a door that leads to a gallery which is also fitted with display windows and a row of video screens showing scenes from the interior of the establishment. At the end of this gallery there is a small patio which is where the true entrance to the shop is found, made out of cast iron.

In the window displays urban and rural scenes are recreated through the use of elaborate decoration in fine detail, including mannequins as characters in their own right. The scenography which is created in the shop windows constitutes an ideal frame for the display of garments, presented in a context which strengthens the image the brand name wishes to get across.

The lighting is with built-in halogen spots distributed across the ceiling, which create a warm and pleasant atmosphere.

The display function extends further than the shop window itself, spreading into the interior, as the display of articles continues intermittently throughout the premises. Corners can be found in which domestic scenes are represented, with mannequins as the characters, or architectural elements belonging to a private house, such as a fireplace shoe display. It is, in short, an original way of overcoming the limits of a window, to convert the interior space into an enormous shop window, capable of reflecting different forms and styles, and different daily situations in which the clothes acquire their own protagonism.

Floor plan of the distribution of the premises, with the two main window displays indicated by arrows.

Above, a view of the glass door which leads to the interior patio; on the left a rural scene, and on the right video screens offering images of the interior of the establishment.

In the shop windows an almost theatrical atmosphere has been created, with minutely worked decorations and a lighting effect which contributes to the perception of a suggestive and attractive atmosphere which invites the passer by to enter the shop and discover the interior.

GIAN MARCO VENTURI

Anna Clerici & Maddalena de Molinari

A view of the shop window from the interior of the shop illustrating the full glazing and the wide door at the entrance. In the top right-hand corner one of the television screens is visible, on which images are projected to attract the attention of the passers by.

On the following page, one of the display counters, of an original glass and steel design, on which the garments are arranged.

GianMarcoVenturi

In the photographs, two views of the arches which dominate the façade of the building, and which perfectly frame the whole of the shop window display.

Access is gained to the premises through two arches belonging to the original structure of the old building which houses the shop. At the top of the arches the old iron railings have been kept, and below, wide glass doors have been installed bearing the name of the establishment, which is also present on a sober metallic plaque which perfectly harmonises with the classic quality of the façade. With this solution, significant alterations to the original structure of the façade were avoided.

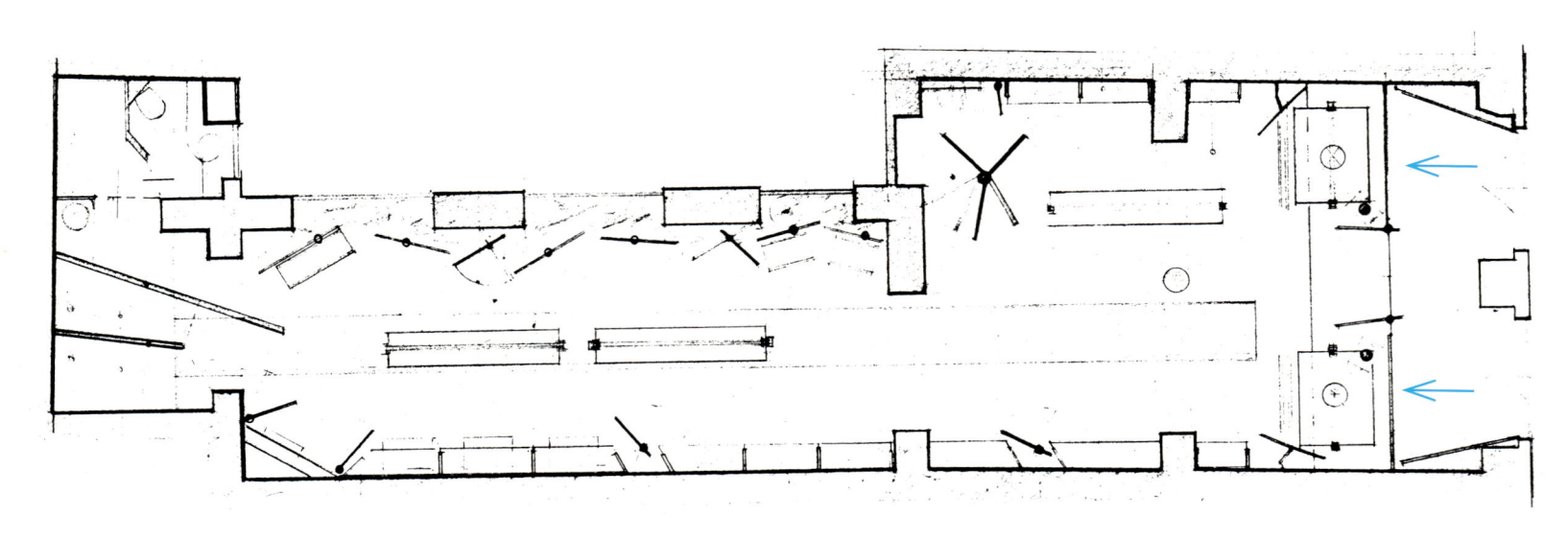

A floor and distribution plan of the premises, with the window display area indicated with arrows.

Behind the glass doors, the shop window properly speaking, glazed to its full height, is found. In the centre a double door opens beside which two low tables have been placed for display purposes. The tables consist of a round leg with a steel crossbar which supports the large square glass top. On this surface the garments and accessories to be displayed can be arranged. Two video screens, on which fashion shows and programmes to stimulate the interest of the public are run, complete the furnishings of the window display.

The window display space is separated from the interior by a low step and two blinds of adjustable length, which filter the interior light. The lighting comes from a series of spots attached to the ceiling by a rail.

Different views of the interior of the premises; the light tones and use of glass and mirrors, increasing the sense of space, are the predominant decorative features. Only a step and blinds of an adjustable length separate the shop window from the rest of the shop.

LOFT

Patrick Frêche

A nocturnal view of the façade and the shop's window displays, emphasising the warmth of the interior lighting contrasted against the dark exterior tones of the premises.

On the following page, garments and complimentary articles displayed on the wooden floor and the mannequins; the direct lighting, based on normal-voltage spots, creates a daring and youthful avant-garde atmosphere.

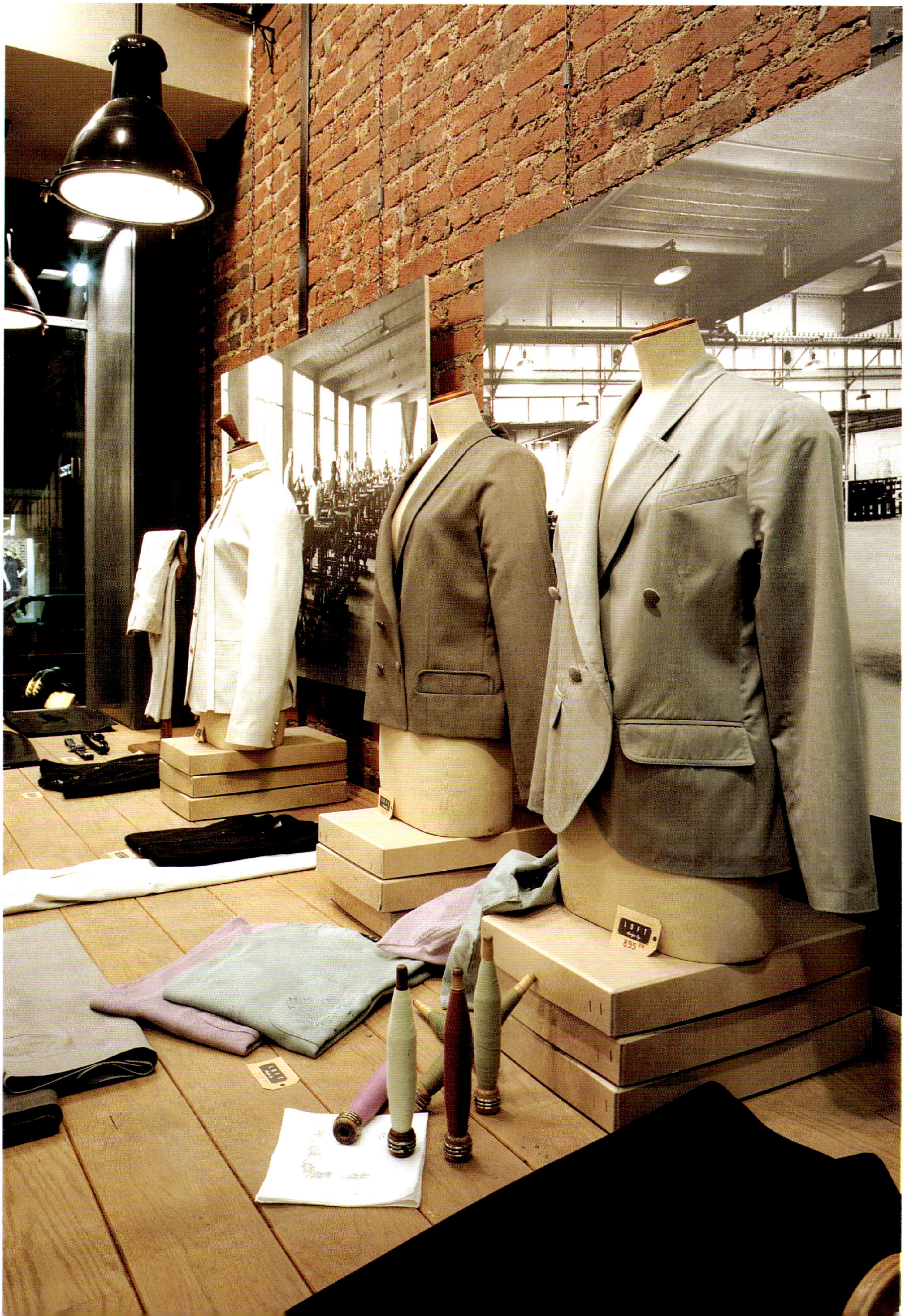

The photographs of famous people combined with the iron latticework creates a highly attractive, original and avant-garde space.

This shop is located in a building which dates back to the time of the construction of the Eiffel Tower; perhaps for this reason the exterior structure of the premises is based on the use of metal. Awnings bearing the company's trademark, which also appears at the top of the façade, overlook the part of the shop window display which gives onto the street.

On the outside of the shop window, metallic structures, combined with wood in dark tones, are predominant, counterpointed by the interior of the window display with its walls of exposed brickwork and warm lighting effect, which create a pleasant and intimate atmosphere. The garments are found in orderly displays, offering the potential customer a carefully selected sample of the different articles. The display is based on clothes hangers and articles draped across the wooden platforms, worn by the mannequins or scattered around them, creating an informal, but at the same time harmonic, air. The decor and the garments form a perfect conjunction, occupying the ground which lies somewhere between the rigour of modernism and the warmth of an authenticity which accurately reflects the commercial image of the brand name.

The dominant tone of the façade and the window displays is greyish blue, painted over wood and iron, giving the space an air which suggests and revives the old traditional Parisian commercial establishments, yet at the same time demonstrating a perfect symbiosis of the classical and the modern. The expression of this idea lies behind the window displays and the decor, reflecting a way of thinking and understanding life.

The harmony of the garments on display draped across the wooden flooring, the exposed brickwork wall on which the black and white photographs are arranged and the characteristic structure of the latticework combine to form of a space which stands out for its great plasticity.

On the right, a front view of the shop's façade.

131

GALTRUCCO

Piero Pinto

A view of the establishment from the exterior. At two thirds of the full height of the windows a metal band is located bearing the name of the establishment, and limiting the visual space of the window display.

On the following page, the interior of the entrance with its L-shaped window, which provides an extended display space. On the left, one of the metallic structures designed as a display support for the different garments, and on the right, the entrance to the interior of the shop flanked by two neoclassical columns.

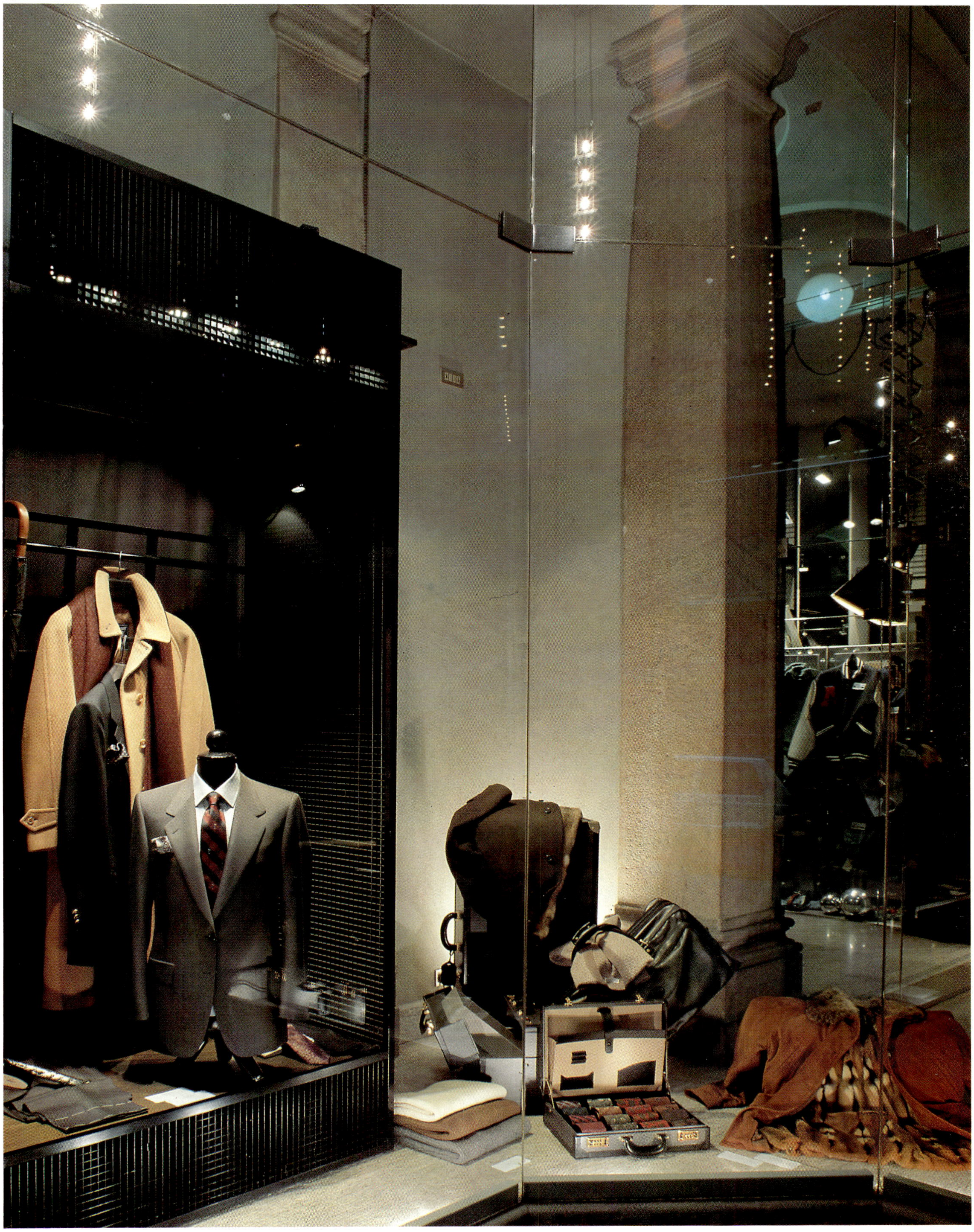

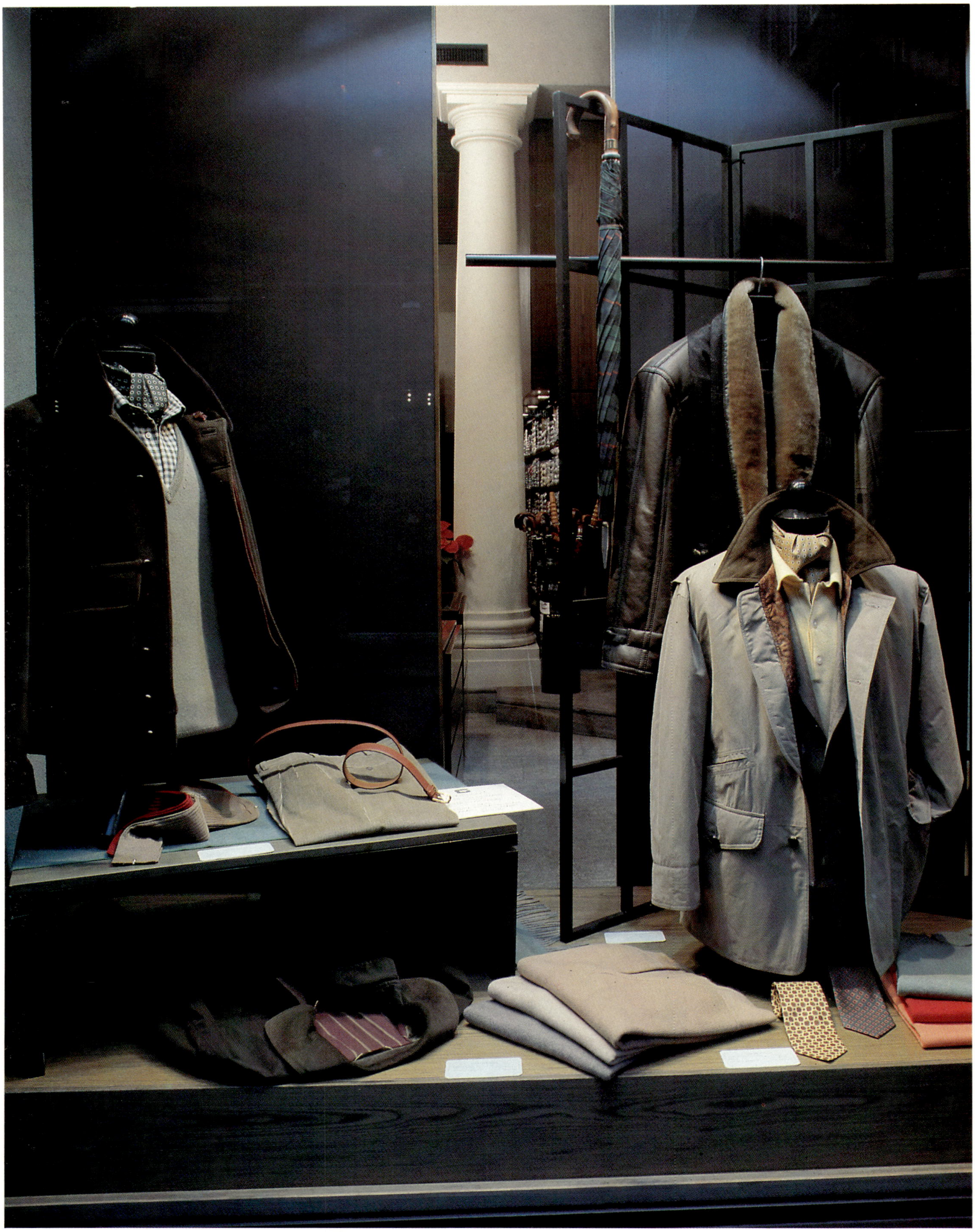

In the project for the interior decoration of this shop the desire to give preeminence to the window display was made evident; the premises give onto the street through four openings, two of which are conventional shop windows connected to the interior of the establishment by means of sliding panels. These openings were completely glazed, but at about two thirds of the full height a dividing metal band was placed, bearing the name of the company and framing the visual space. Inside the window this limitation is imposed by the metallic latticework which also serves as a support for the halogen lamps.

In the other two openings between the premises and the street the metallic band has been maintained, announcing the name of the establishment and giving visual continuity to the façade, but the openings are left as accesses to the new display space.

Having crossed this threshold into the rectangular entrance with its two glazed walls there is an extensive collection of articles on display. Iron latticework structures were created as display counters and placed both in the window displays facing the street and in the entrance itself, their avant-garde design contrasting with the neoclassical architectural elements inside the shop.

On the fourth side, access is gained to the sales area properly speaking. The façade is in this way introduced into the interior space of the shop and, at the same time, the display space is extended, creating an atmosphere of transition between the street and the shop which is perfectly conceived for the relaxed contemplation of the products on display.

On the previous page, an illustration of the ordered display of articles forming sober compositions of garments and complementary accessories arranged on the floor, accompanied by mannequins and hangers.

Above, a view of the window display from the interior, limited at the rear by sliding panels and above by a metal latticework which supports a series of halogen spots. Below, partial view of the entrance.

ARAMIS

Mario Framis & Juan Flores

Partial view of one of the window displays, where the clothes are presented on a platform which is elevated to a height that is more accessible for viewing by the public. The composition is based on the coordination of clothes and accessories, as in the photograph, in which jackets, trousers, and shirts are accompanied by a leather wallet, shoes and a safari hat.

Above, one of the glass display cases in the interior, in which clothes and matching accessories are displayed.

An original wooden display cabinet whose multiple compartments allow for the displaying of different products, each being granted its own importance.

The shop has three openings onto the street, one a completely glazed window, one a display window and the third remaining permanently open as the access to an entrance which is also a display area. The latter two openings have a gold trimmed plaque the centre of which is occupied by the company's trademark, which is also gold coloured. The name of the establishment is printed on the two awnings and on a plaque inlaid in the column which separates the two openings.

All of the shop windows have been lined with fine woods, and the garments and complementary articles are presented either directly, on a platform which is elevated to a more accessible height where they can be seen by the public, or through the use of wooden mannequins of various sizes. The lighting is based on spots built into the ceiling which project ambient light, and are complemented by other lights directed onto the garments in order to emphasise their colours and textures.

In the lobby, the window display flooring is parquet, as is the wainscot on the green fabric-clad walls. The atmosphere of serene classicism, which constitutes one of the most important elements of the image of the brand name Aramis, can be perceived before entering the establishment and continues in the interior of the shop.

A view of the exterior of the premises, with one of the openings used as a display window and the other leading to the entrance, also used for display.

On the next page, a view of the enormous window which gives onto the façade, and which is completely glazed, the walls being clad with the same fine wood which is predominant in the interior. The trademark is screen printed onto the glass, and the spots hanging from the ceiling and attached to the walls complete the perfect frame for this display featuring two suits and their respective complementary accessories.

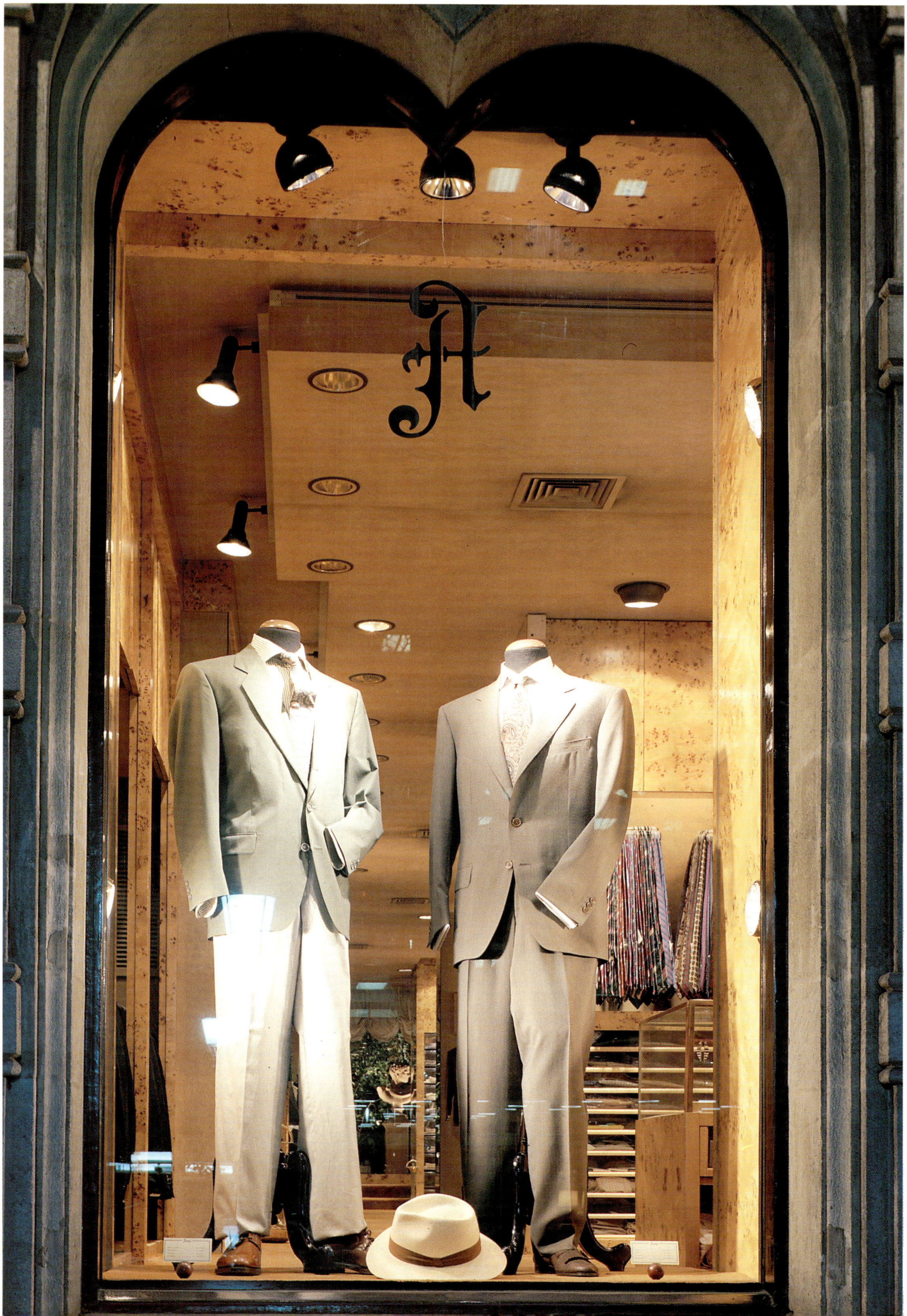

Centimetre

Cezar Rinalducci

On the previous page, partial view of the window display, in which a variety of geometrical structures are used as supports for the garments. The predominance of the colour red, the prime representative of Soviet paraphernalia, is evident in all of the display areas.

The most outstanding aspect of this shop is its specialisation in an aesthetic and a product with such strong connotations: the Soviet brand of clothes. The key idea is the exploitation of the Russian phenomenon as a leitmotif for a series of fashion collections. The image of Gorbachev has been used and a complete merchandising operation has been established, planned down to the very last detail.

The shop window display is very informal, as is the fashion style contained in it, the predominant element being Soviet paraphernalia. The decorative elements are advertising gadgets designed by the Soviet brand, based on the visual wealth and tradition offered by Soviet graphic imagery since the Revolution. For example, the typography is extremely attractive and novel, due to its striking differences from Western typography, and it is used skilfully as a complement to the rest of the image, in both small and large-scale formats.

A good advertising tactic is the profusion of visual signs which subconsciously seduce the customer, enveloping him in a particular symbology. Geometric forms are employed with flair, and a rich and varied collection of symbols and logos are used which within a Western context have surprising results. The colour red is ubiquitous, and is repeatedly to be found in a variety of combinations. Lights built into the ceiling complete the atmosphere which has been created as a reflection of a corporate image aimed at a young public who like to follow fashion by adding a characteristic touch to their style which in a way reflects the uncertainties of the times we live in.

Soviet typography is used as a novel graphic means of awakening the curiosity of the public through the disparity between Cyrillic script and the Western alphabet.

An exterior view of the premises, with the entrance located at the angle formed by the two shop windows.

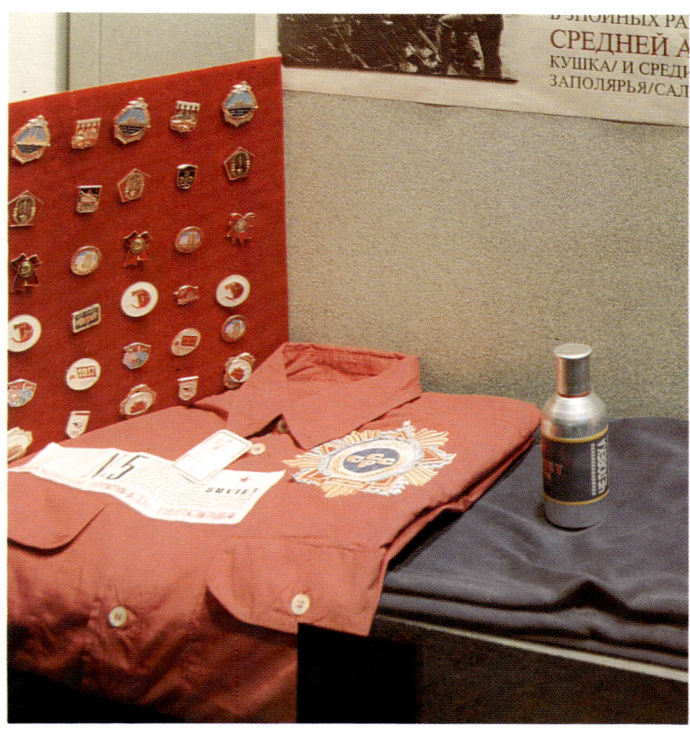

The use of graphic and symbolic elements related to Soviet ideology is taken to the limit and repeated with insistency, in order to create a genuine, and real, atmosphere.

On the following page, the entrance to the inside of the establishment, overlooked by a granite plaque with the name of the shop engraved on the stone. Two plaques, similar to this but longer, are to be found over the main shop windows.

CENTIMETRE

REPLAY

Stefania Leonardi & Rodolfo Dacomo

On the previous page, a view of the window display from the interior, access to it being direct, without any physical separation between the two spaces. The various decorative elements, furnishings and decor contribute to the creation of the factory look.

Above, front view of the entrance. Between the floors of the shop, the name is displayed in majestic towering letters cut in steel. As can be seen in the other photographs, the chromatic richness of the garments has been made one of the characteristics of the decor of the shop.

This shop sells its products to a male public interested in sports and informal clothing. Elements characteristic of industrial architecture have been used in the window dressing, such as original supports consisting of steel conveyer belts in constant movement; from these, shirts and jackets are hung on classical hangers, while on the parquet flooring a wide range of garments and complementary accessories are arranged.

From the window displays, the interior space is limited by the inclusion of rusty iron crane jibs which mark out the display area.

Particular attention has been paid to the selection of the materials and the treatment of all of the decorative elements. The American

oak and rusty iron have been aged and contrast with the chromed aluminium spots, contributing to the creation of an atmosphere redolent of a manufacturing environment. The lighting is provided by spots which bestow a clean, dynamic ambience transmitting great vitality.

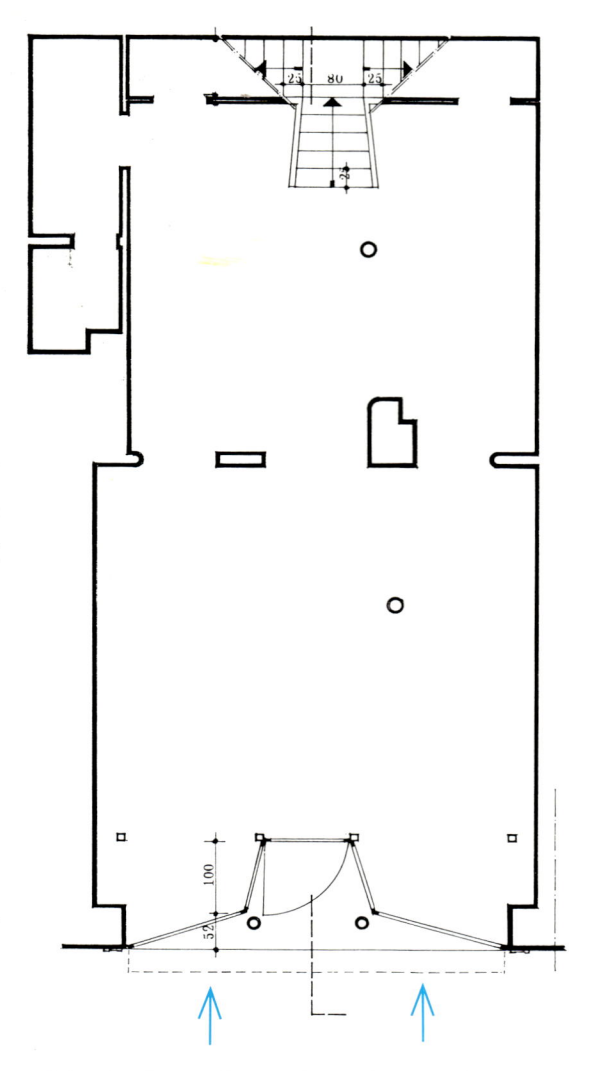

Floor plans of the shop's two floors: above, the ground floor with the window displays indicated by arrows; and on the right, the first floor.

On the following page, a display counter made of wood and metal; the stepped arrangement allows for the display of different clothes and complementary articles.

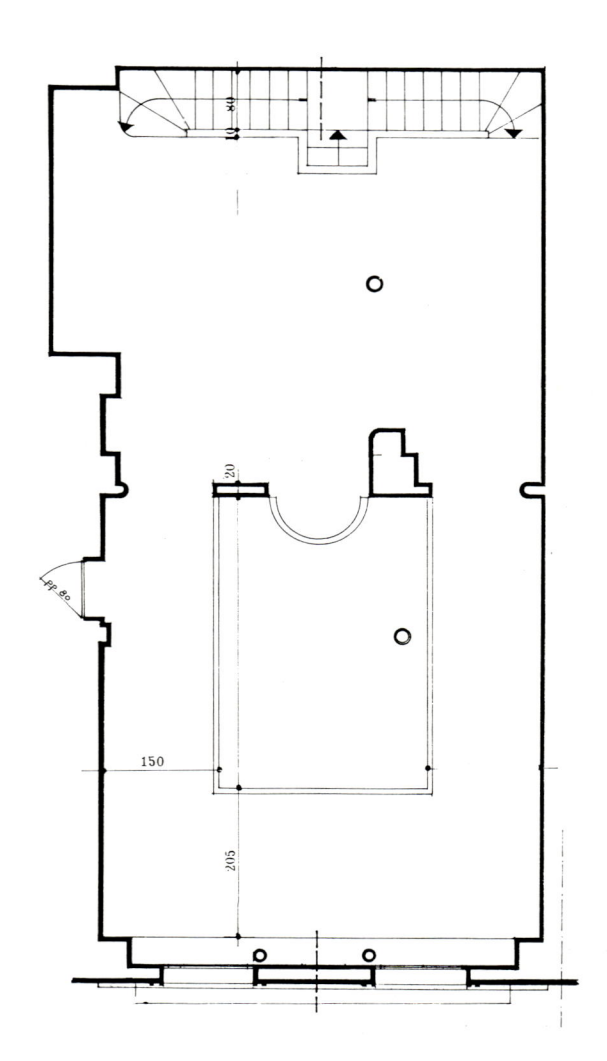

146

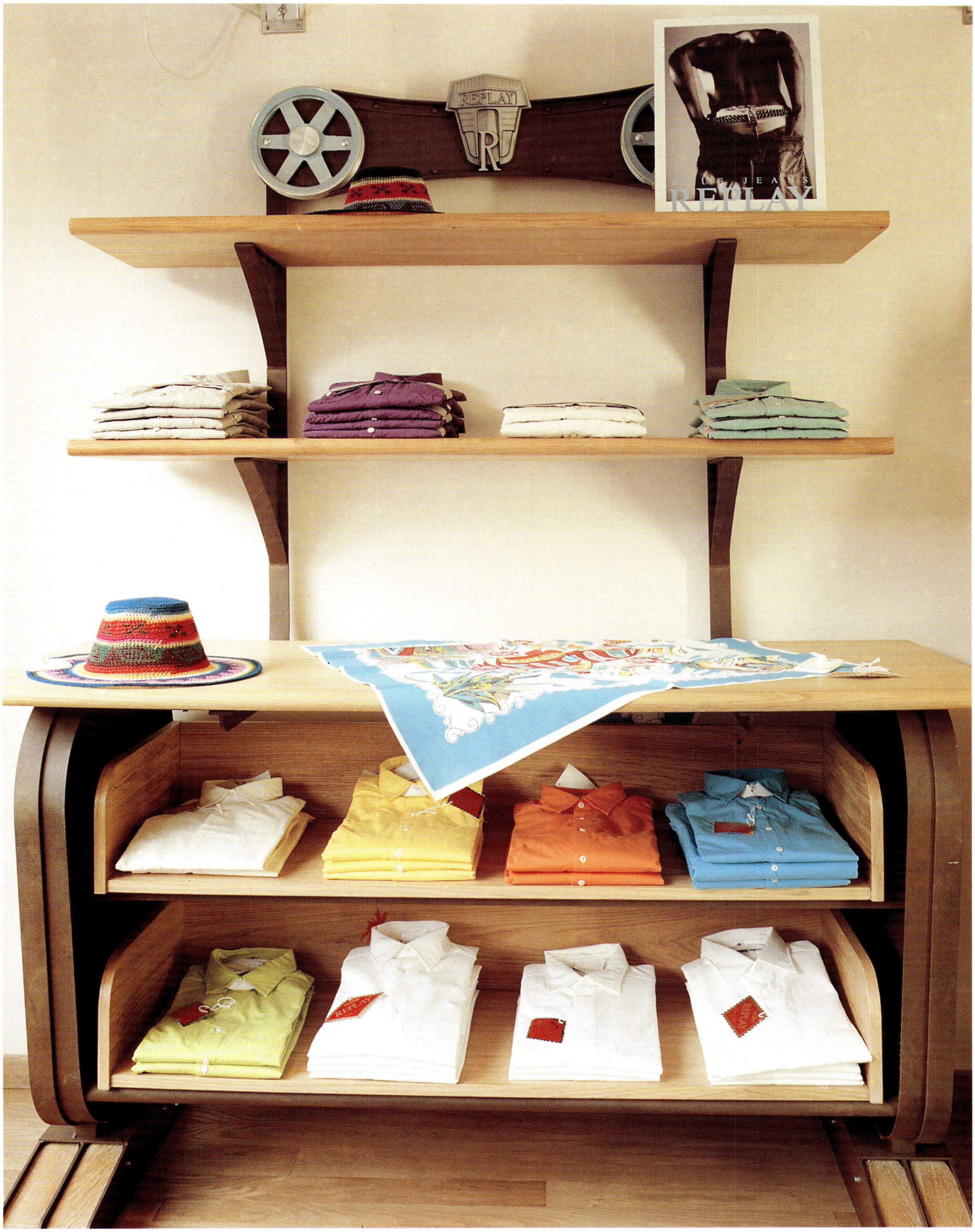
REPLAY
REPLAY

OLIVIER STRELLI

Michèle Kuborn

Despite the ample space available for window dressing, the choice was made not to occupy it all, but to mount limited yet precise displays. The arrangement of the mannequins confers a high degree of realism to the display image.

On the following page, a mannequin dressed in red is distanced from the others by an empty space, which nevertheless manages to preserve its compositional balance.

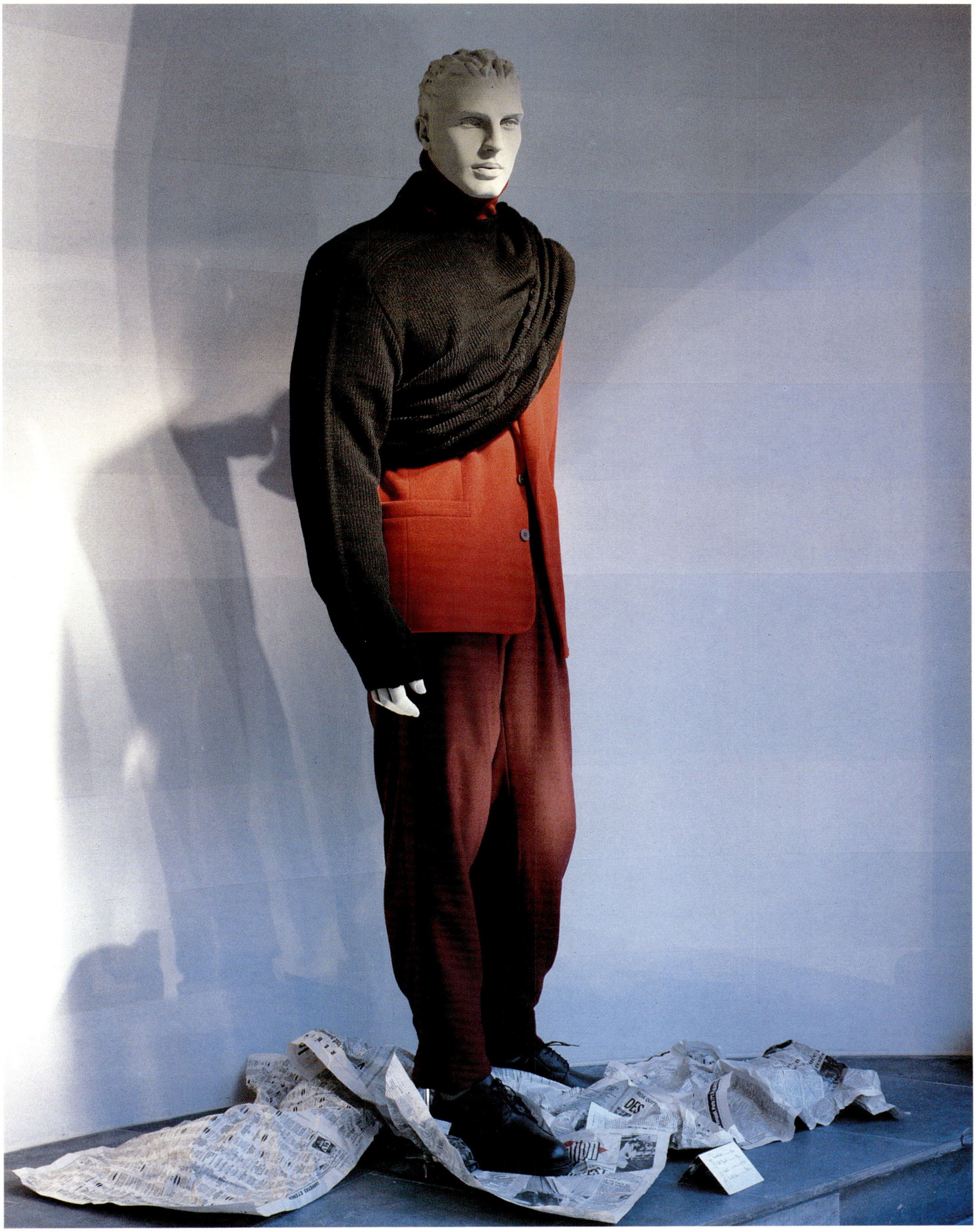

150

The image offered by the shop is in tune with the style of clothes which is sold there, up-to-date, avant-garde and over-the-top fashion. In the window display the style is shown by means of totally figurative mannequins which evoke an archetype of modern man, resolute and liberal.

The display philosophy is based on simplicity and strength; few decorative resources are used, but with great flair. The mannequins themselves, with their dynamics and expression of movement and decision, are symbolic of a complete lifestyle. Groups have been created according to the type of clothing, or in terms of a certain chromatic range. In the window display, four mannequin wearing clothes in grey tones create a compositional unity, while further back another, dressed in red, appears to be following them at a distance.

The single focus of all their looks, directed towards the access door, appears to dare the customer to enter while at the same time intimidating him. They are urban men on an opaque grey flooring covered in scraps of screwed up paper, and yet they are impeccably dressed.

The window display is separated from the interior of the shop by a curved brick wall which contrasts with the straight lines and symmetry of the rest of the establishment.

The lighting is provided by directional halogen spots, hanging from the ceiling, and from other smaller spots located at floor level, producing deliberate shadows which multiply the forms.

On the previous page and below, two different shots of the arrangement of the mannequins, whose looks are all directed towards the entrance as if inviting the passers by to come in.

Some articles of exceptional quality are displayed in the interior in glass display cases such as the one shown in the photo.

Emporio Armani

Giancarlo Ortelli

A great deal of the interior is set aside for display purposes. The clothing and complementary accessories are displayed in wardrobes, glass display cases and on light-toned wooden shelves, with a predominance of straight lines and structural symmetry. In the photograph, an arrangement of jackets, trousers and shirts in a wardrobe with sliding doors obeys a strictly controlled display symmetry.

All of the complements are arranged on shelves following a chromatic distribution of great visual force.

Views of the exterior of the premises during the day and when lit at night. The window displays are harmoniously integrated into the style of the XVII-century façade.

Below, an original display counter for ties and complements. On the following page, one of the window displays; the white backdrop is made up of panels which separate the display area from the interior and which help to emphasise the protagonism of the displayed clothes.

The boutique is located in a building designed with the aesthetic features which were the dominant style of the XVII century, in Place Vendôme, in Paris. Both the shop windows and the entrance are enclosed by the stilted arches of the façade, showing absolute faithfulness to the original architectural structures. These in turn are highlighted thanks to the dark profile which frames them, crowned by an eagle, the company's symbol, directly contrasting with the white of the panels.

The shop window displays individually present a scenic combination which is back-framed by a structure in three parts, a trio of panels forming a U-shape. The display of articles on the coupled supports, which simulate fully dressed men and women also include an occasional complementary accessory, yet always integrated into the whole. The composition is simple, free of all surplus elements, always representative of a deliberate and perfectly integrated group. This is a true reflection of one of the ideological guidelines of the world of Armani: the force of simplicity.

Natural materials are used for the supports, light colours always dominating, creating a sober and elegant context to which the lighting adds a touch of delicacy.

Each detail has been studied to express what is in reality not merely a space destined for sales, but the interpretation of an integrated lifestyle.

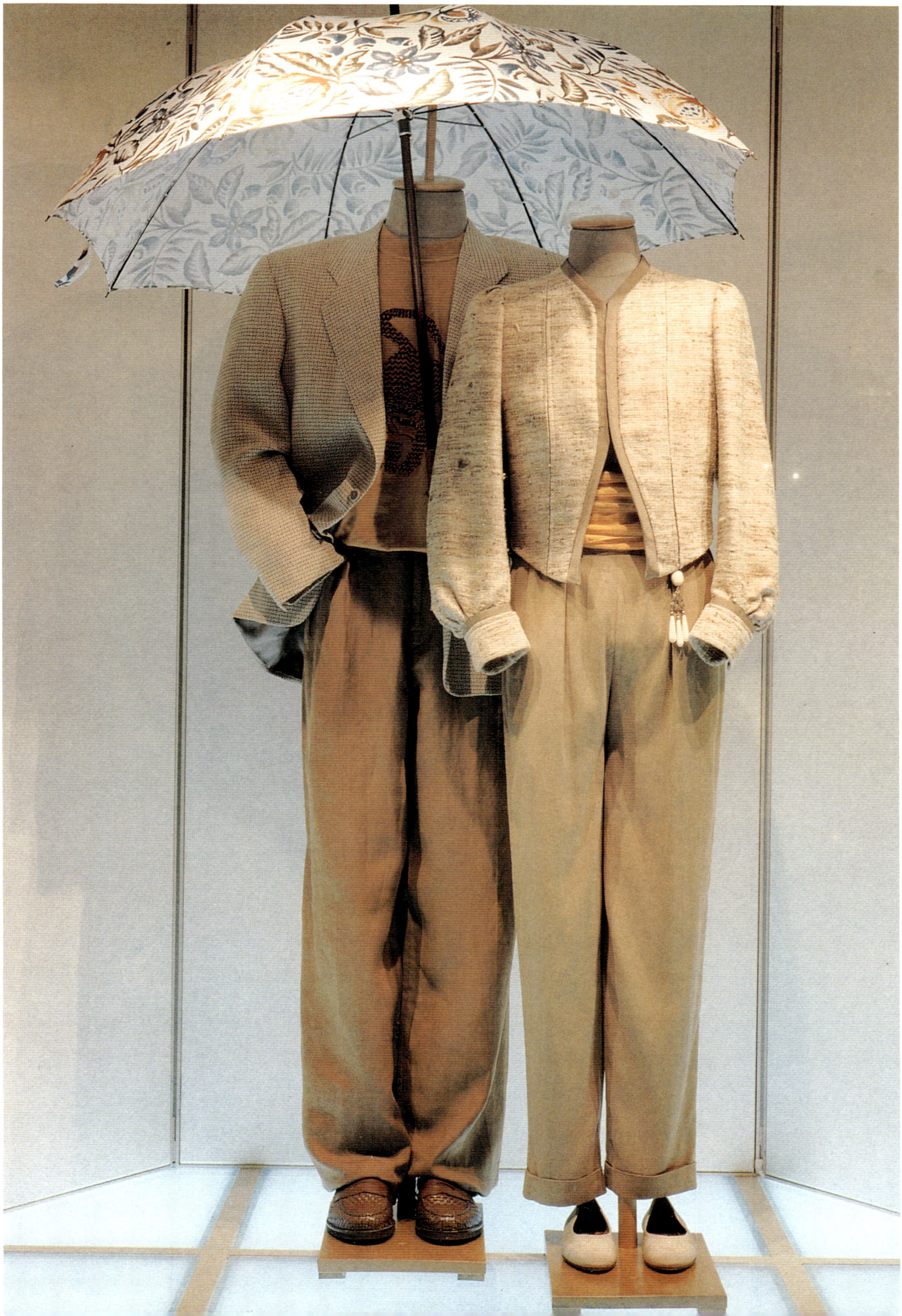

AZUL

Isabel García Tapia

A perspective of the granite façade and the exterior of the shop, shown to advantage by lighting which emphasises and highlights the worth of the company's trademark.

On the following page, a composition of great richness, yet in which each of the elements on display acquires a specific independence. The contrast between the vertical and the horizontal arrangement serves as a means of attracting the attention of potential customers.

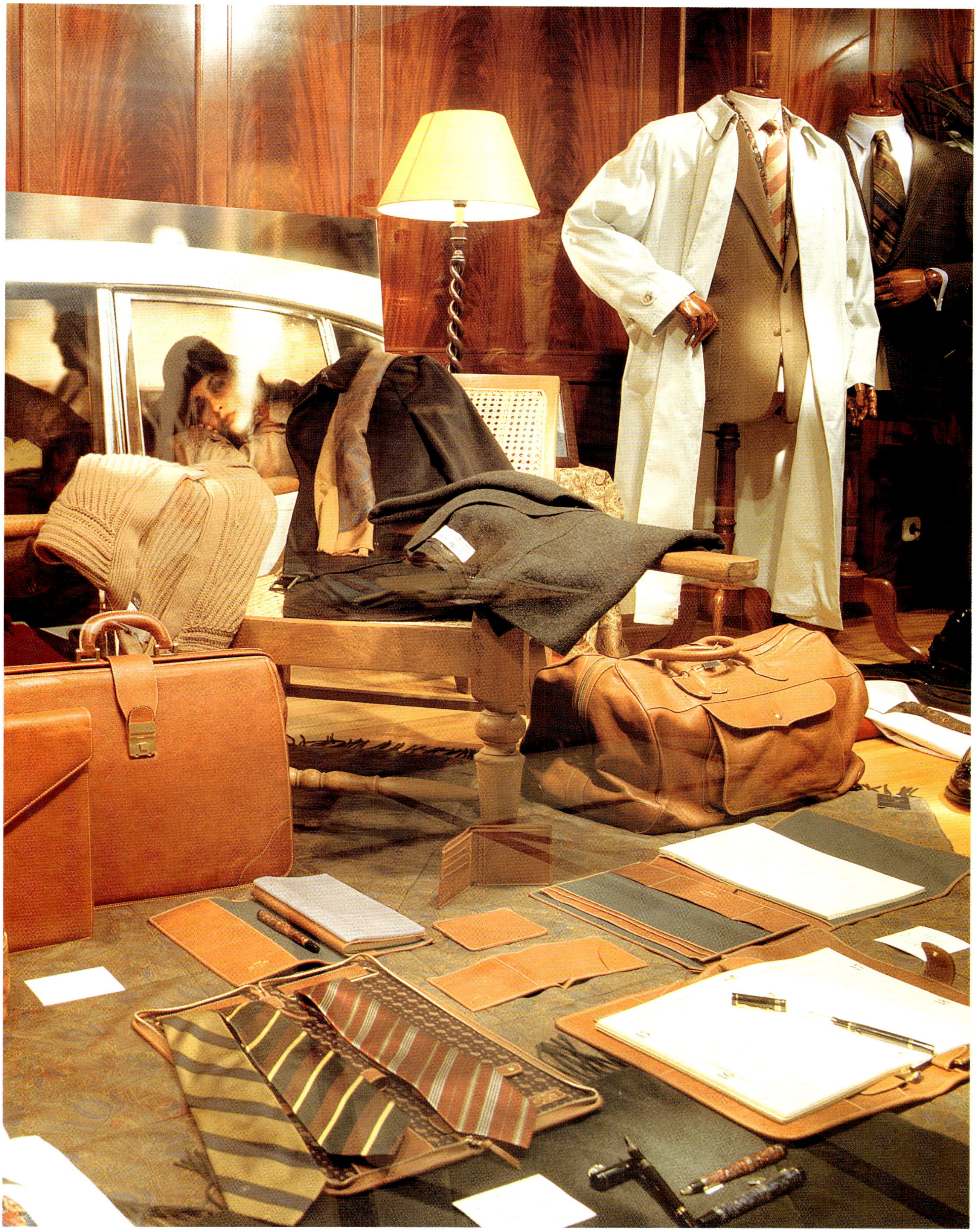

Access

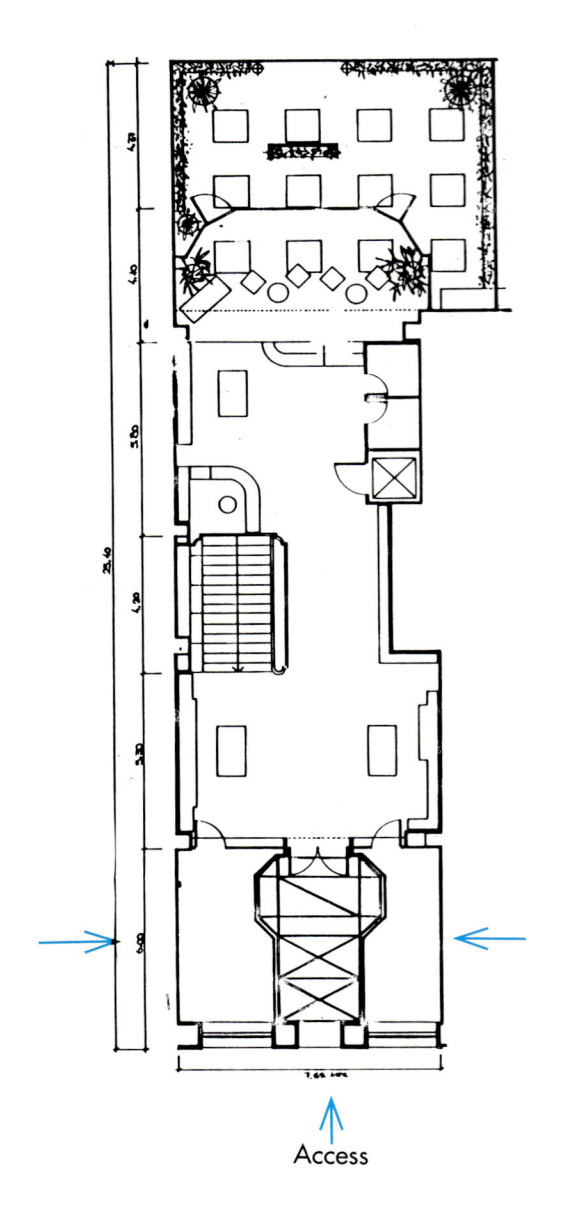

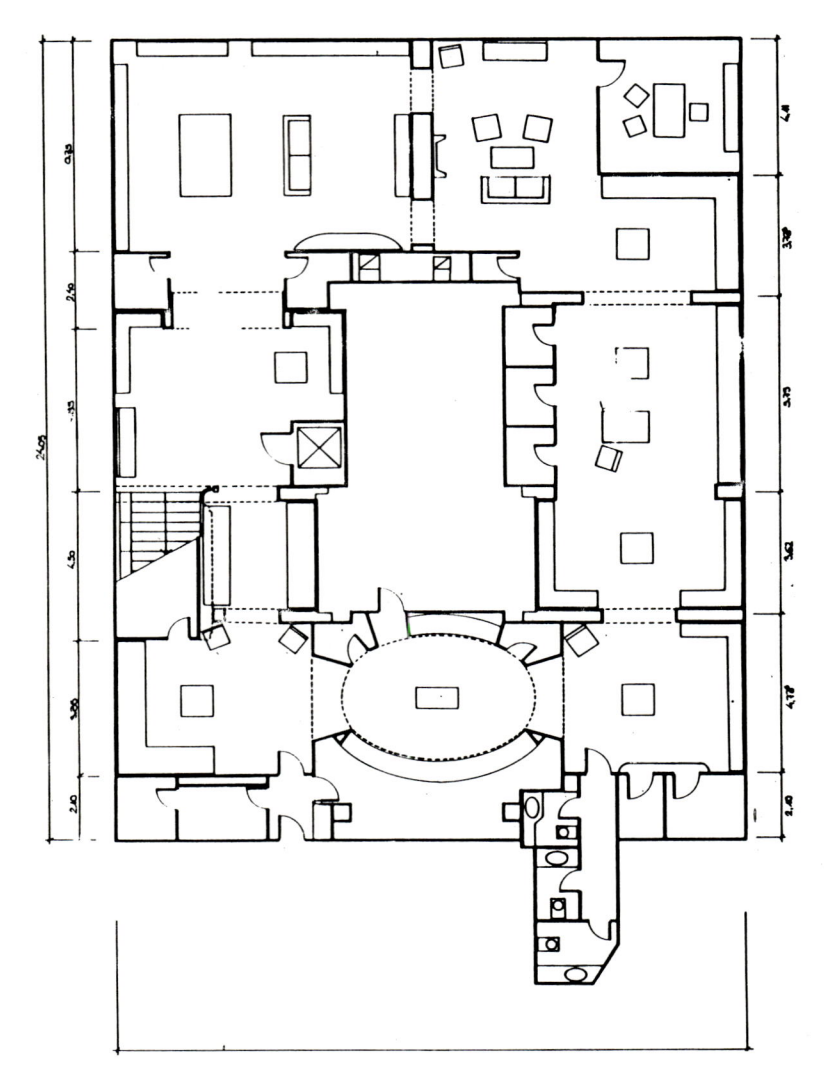

Floor plan of the floors which make up the premises and their distribution; the window displays are indicated by arrows.

This establishment offers a wide range of select products for men in an atmosphere of quality and luxury. The narrow, discreet granite façade does not give any clues as to the richness of the interior.

Thus the shop window is extended inwards through an elegant atrium in which the geometric designs in the marble paving are reflected on the ceiling. The wooden flooring is treated as a display support element for the shop windows, and the garments are draped in an ordered fashion across this, arranged in groups or worn by the classical mannequins.

At the foot of the two display windows which flank the atrium, and which define the access door to the premises, two slabs of grey granite repeat the shop's trademark and the year of its inauguration.

The furnishings used for the display of the different products follows a classical line, with the use of wood as the base material. The lighting is provided by directional halogen spots and the chromatics is in predominantly brown and ochre tones, contributing to the creation of an atmosphere which transmits a sense of elegance and comfort to the observer.

Azul could be defined as a shop inspired in the classical English style, brought up to date by a Mediterranean feel which adds a strong dash of vitality and modernity to its intrinsic elegance.

The granite slabs impress upon the customers the name of the shop and give the window display yet another classical and elegant reference.

Some of the complements are given prominence in the interior through being displayed in glass cases, lit by diminutive points of light.